Ricle

ALTERNATIVE ECONOMIC INDICATORS

Victor Anderson

London and New York

First published 1991 by Routledge
11 New Fetter Lane, London EC4P 4EE

Simultaneously published in the USA and Canada
by Routledge
a division of Routledge, Chapman and Hall, Inc.
29 West 35th Street, New York, NY 10001

Typeset in Palatino by
Selectmove Ltd, London
Printed and bound in Great Britain by
Biddles Ltd, Guildford and King's Lynn

British Library Cataloguing in Publication Data
Anderson, Victor
Alternative economic indicators.
1. Economic conditions. Policies
I. Title
330.9
ISBN 0–415–04163–5
ISBN 0–415–04164–3 pbk

Library of Congress Cataloging-in-Publication Data
Anderson, Victor, 1952–
Alternative economic indicators / Victor Anderson.
p.   cm.
Includes bibliographical references and index.
ISBN 0–415–04163–5. -- ISBN 0–415–04164–3
1. National income--Accounting.   2. Economic indicators.
3. Social indicators. 4. Economic policy. 5. Economic development
I. Title.
HC79.I5A5   1991
338.9--dc20
90–26752
CIP

CONTENTS

Acknowledgements

Introduction

1 THE GROWTH DEBATE   1

2 THE ORIGINS OF NATIONAL INCOME
   ACCOUNTING   16

3 PROBLEMS OF NATIONAL INCOME ACCOUNTING   21

4 POSSIBLE REFORMS IN NATIONAL INCOME
   ACCOUNTING   33

5 GROWTH AND PROGRESS   42

6 THE GOOD INDICATOR   48

7 SOCIAL INDICATORS   55

8 ENVIRONMENTAL INDICATORS   65

9 DATA FOR FOURTEEN MAJOR COUNTRIES   75

10 CONCLUSIONS   86

Notes and references   96

Index   102

ACKNOWLEDGEMENTS

I would like to thank James Robertson, and my other colleagues in the New Economics Foundation, without whose support and advice this book could not have been written. I would also like to thank the Environmental Research Trust for the financial support which has enabled me to write it.

My thanks to the following people for their comments and advice: Frankie Ashton, John Ashton, Mike Bell, Trevor Blackwell, Frank Bracho, David Cope, John Corkindale, Tim Crabtree, John Davis, Paul Ekins, John Hatfield, Mayer Hillman, Michael Jacobs, Ian Miles, Ward Morehouse, Roger Pritchard, Joan Rawlinson, Andrea Ries, Hans Singer, Michael J Weatherley, Pat Wooding; and the participants in a seminar on indicators called by President Perez of Venezuela. Chapter 8 is based partly on information provided by Norman Myers.

Victor Anderson
London

The address of the New Economics Foundation is:
Universal House, 88–94 Wentworth Street, London E1 7SA.

INTRODUCTION

Modern economies are highly complex but the thinking which guides politicians is often extremely simple. One of the simple ideas which has bewitched politicians has been the concept of 'maximizing economic growth'. This has become the central long-term economic policy objective of most governments.

There are other objectives as well, of course, and these may conflict with achieving maximum growth. Nevertheless, economic growth is in itself generally held to be necessarily good, and the more of it the better. As the most important objective of the economic policies of most governments, whatever their political persuasion, the aim of 'maximizing economic growth' has enormous influence on their thinking and decision-making.

In recent years it has come in for increasing criticism, particularly from supporters of green politics, who have often argued the opposite view, that growth is in itself necessarily bad, particularly for the environment. However, one question which has not often been answered at all persuasively by the critics of economic growth is this: 'What would you put in its place?' If the maximization of growth is to be rejected as the central aim of economic policy, what aim should replace it? That question was the starting-point for this book.

One of the strengths which 'economic growth' has as an idea is that it can be measured statistically. A persuasive alternative to growth probably has to be measurable too. This turns the debate about the aims of economic policy into one about indicators, which are the means of measuring whether or not the aims are being achieved.

My initial objective in writing this book was to identify a single statistic which could dethrone and replace the rate of growth of gross national product (GNP) as the principal indicator. I have not been able to find one. Instead, I argue for a whole set of indicators, rather than a single one which can play all the roles which GNP is supposed to play.

Nevertheless, I have tried to be very selective in my choice of indicators. The book does not attempt to set out a comprehensive system of indicators to measure all aspects of life. It attempts instead to argue for the choice of a small number of indicators as being the most significant and the most important to have information about, if we want to measure the real progress of an economy, instead of the illusory 'progress' often represented by growth in GNP.

The book starts by looking at the debate between the advocates and opponents of continued economic growth, and at the importance of that debate for the emergence of green politics. Chapter 2 is a brief investigation into the origins of gross national product and the national income accounting system it is part of. Chapter 3 presents a detailed critique of the claims popularly made for GNP. Chapter 4 examines proposals which have been put forward for modifying GNP in various ways, by means of additions, subtractions, etc. It concludes that these proposals, whilst often useful, do not go far enough and that a different approach is needed.

The basis of such an approach is set out in chapter 5, which argues for economies to be evaluated by indicators measuring their social and environmental consequences, not by purely financial measurements of economic progress. Chapter 6 looks into the question of what, in general terms, would make a good set of indicators.

Chapters 7 and 8 argue for specific priority indicators. Chapter 7 is about indicators concerned with people and their living standards; chapter 8 is about indicators of the environment and natural resources.

Chapter 9 presents statistics for sixteen recommended priority indicators for fourteen different countries. Chapter 10 draws some conclusions, both about indicators and about the state of the world.

1

THE GROWTH DEBATE

THE ANTI-GROWTH CASE

A Blueprint for Survival

In January 1972, *The Ecologist* magazine, edited by Edward Goldsmith, published a special issue called *A Blueprint for Survival*. This declared that 'The principal defect of the industrial way of life with its ethos of expansion is that it is not sustainable. . . Radical change is both necessary and inevitable because the present increases in human numbers and per capita consumption, by disrupting ecosystems and depleting resources, are undermining the very foundations of survival.'[1]

Central to the analysis in the *Blueprint* was the question of economic growth and its environmental impact: 'A distinguished group of scientists, who came together for a "Study of Critical Environmental Problems" (SCEP) under the auspices of the Massachusetts Institute of Technology, state in their report the clear need for a means of measuring this impact, and have coined the term "ecological demand", which they define as "a summation of all man's demands on the environment, such as the extraction of resources and the return of wastes". *Gross domestic product (GDP)*, which is population multiplied by material standard of living, appears to provide the most convenient measure of ecological demand.'[1] 'It should go without saying that the world cannot accommodate this continued increase in ecological demand. *Indefinite* growth of whatever type cannot be sustained by *finite* resources. This is the nub of the environmental predicament.'[2]

The authors then set out in detail their case against indefinite growth. Looking back, their greatest mistake was the inclusion of a graph (on page 7) showing the impact on mineral reserves of a continuation in their current rates of use, and a continuation in

1

the recent rate of growth in their use. This projection was widely taken as a 'prediction' that silver, gold, mercury, and lead would all run out within twenty years – something which clearly has not happened. This graph in particular, and the argument about resource depletion generally, became the main target for critics of the *Blueprint*. Although the critics were widely believed to have won the argument, there were other aspects of the *Blueprint* which received less attention and which now appear to have been far more valid, such as their analyses of pollution, soil erosion, deforestation, and global warming.

The *Blueprint* also presented a social case against growth: 'There is every reason to believe that the social ills at present afflicting our society – increasing crime, delinquency, vandalism, alcoholism as well as drug addiction – are closely related and are symptoms of the breakdown of our cultural pattern which in turn is an aspect of the disintegration of our society. These tendencies can only be accentuated by further demographic and economic growth. . . . It is the cause itself, unchecked economic and demographic growth, that must be treated.'[3]

The *Blueprint* set out a series of policies for ensuring that this would be done, and announced the launching of a new organization, Movement for Survival. Although this organization never really started, discussions about it contributed to the formation of People, which became the Ecology Party, which later changed its name to the Green Party. The *Blueprint* became a major influence on green thinking.

The Limits to Growth

In the same year as the *Blueprint* was published in Britain and the United Nations Conference on the Environment was held in Sweden (1972), *The Limits to Growth* was published in the USA. This gave an account of a study of the future of the world. Commissioned by the Club of Rome, the study was carried out by a research team based at the Massachusetts Institute of Technology under the directorship of Dr Dennis Meadows. It centred on a computer model consisting of a series of equations for relationships between key variables such as the level of population, food supply, and arable land area.

2

The conclusions of the study were:

1 If the present growth trends in world population, industriali-zation, pollution, food production, and resource depletion continue unchanged, the limits to growth on this planet will be reached sometime within the next one hundred years. The most probable result will be a rather sudden and uncontrollable decline in both population and industrial capacity.

2 It is possible to alter these growth trends and to establish a condition of ecological and economic stability that is sustainable far into the future. The state of global equilibrium could be designed so that the basic material needs of each person on earth are satisfied and each person has an equal opportunity to realize his individual human potential.

3 If the world's people decide to strive for this second outcome rather than the first, the sooner they begin working to attain it, the greater will be their chances of success.[4]

The Limits to Growth explains the different projected outcomes which were produced by varying the assumptions included in the computer model. With 'no major change in the physical, economic, or social relationships that have historically governed the development of the world system', the outcome is: 'Food, industrial output, and population grow exponentially until the rapidly diminishing resource base forces a slowdown in industrial growth. . . . Population growth is finally halted by a rise in the death rate due to decreased food and medical services.'[5] On the assumption that 'new discoveries or advances in technology . . . double the amount of resources economically available',[6] industrial output will reach a higher level, but: 'The larger industrial plant releases pollution at such a rate, how-ever, that the environmental pollution absorption mechanisms become saturated. Pollution rises very rapidly, causing an immediate increase in the death rate and a decline in food production.'[7] A further variation, reducing the amount of pol-lution generated per unit of industrial output, allows 'population and industry to grow until the limit of arable land is reached'.[8] Whether it is halted by resource depletion, pollution, lack of land to grow sufficient food, or (preferably) by voluntary choices, 'the growth phase' of human history will end within the next 100 years.[9]

The 'growth' referred to in *The Limits to Growth* is primarily of two sorts – growth in population and growth in industrial output. Food output and services output are given as separate variables, and it is industrial output which is seen as having the closest connections with resource depletion and pollution. At various points in the book, however, figures for GNP and GNP per capita are quoted in a way which implies that the authors assume that what is true of industrial output growth is true of economic growth in general.[10]

The Limits to Growth concludes by advocating a 'state of global equilibrium' in which population and capital stock are both constant, 'with the forces tending to increase or decrease them in a carefully controlled balance'.[11] 'Every day of continued exponential growth brings the world system closer to the ultimate limits to that growth. A decision to do nothing is a decision to increase the risk of collapse.'[12]

Small is Beautiful

Small is Beautiful, by Dr E. F. Schumacher, was published in 1973. Like the *Blueprint* and *The Limits to Growth* the previous year, it argues against unlimited growth primarily on environmental grounds, but adds a social and religious philosophy of its own: 'the modern world, shaped by modern technology, finds itself involved in three crises simultaneously. First, human nature revolts against inhuman technological, organisational, and political patterns, which it experiences as suffocating and debilitating; second, the living environment which supports human life aches and groans and gives signs of partial break-down; and, third, it is clear . . . that the inroads being made into the world's non-renewable resources, particularly those of fossil fuels, are such that serious bottlenecks and virtual exhaustion loom ahead in the quite foreseeable future. . . . What is quite clear is that a way of life that bases itself on materialism, i.e. on permanent, limitless expansionism in a finite environment, cannot last long.'[13] 'There has never been a time, in any society in any part of the world, without its sages and teachers to challenge materialism and plead for a different order of priorities. . . . Today, however, this message reaches us not solely from the sages and saints but

4

from the actual course of physical events. It speaks to us in the language of terrorism, genocide, breakdown, pollution, exhaustion.'[14]

Economic growth is a central problem, but is itself a consequence of the wrong approach to life: 'economic growth, which viewed from the point of view of economics, physics, chemistry and technology, has no discernable limit, must necessarily run into decisive bottlenecks when viewed from the point of view of the environmental scientist. An attitude to life which seeks fulfilment in the single-minded pursuit of wealth – in short, materialism – does not fit into this world, because it contains within itself no limiting principle, while the environment in which it is placed is strictly limited.'[15]

Economics deserves some of the blame for this state of affairs. It has established 'uneconomic' as one of the most damning criticisms that can be made of anything, and yet 'the judgements of economics . . . are necessarily and methodically narrow . . . they are based on a definition of cost which excludes all "free goods", that is to say, the entire God-given environment, except for those parts of it that have been privately appropriated. This means that an activity can be economic although it plays hell with the environment, and that a competing activity, if at some cost it protects and conserves the environment, will be uneconomic.'[16]

The book's discussions of decentralization ('small is beautiful') and intermediate technology ('technology with a human face') proved to be extremely influential contributions to the thinking of the environmental movement. Dr Schumacher was active in environmental politics as the founder of the Intermediate Technology Development Group and President of the Soil Association.

Like the *Blueprint* and *The Limits to Growth*, *Small is Beautiful* does not discuss the technicalities of gross national product calculations. None of these three publications is particularly interested in GNP as such. They are concerned with the much larger phenomenon which they all call 'growth'. GNP just happens to be, for them, one way of measuring it. There were other writers – most notably Dr E. J. Mishan in *The Costs of Economic Growth* (1967) and Fred Hirsch in *Social Limits to Growth* (1977) – who did discuss GNP specifically (I shall discuss some of the points they made in chapter 3), but that was not the main emphasis of the most influential contributions to the 'anti-growth' side of the argument. For mainstream economists, however, economic growth is *defined* as growth in GNP, and so when they entered the debate to defend economic growth against its critics, they placed far more emphasis than the critics had on GNP specifically. They also challenged the predictions and projections of the environmental 'doomsters'.

THE PRO-GROWTH RESPONSE

A politician's response

At the time of the publication of *A Blueprint for Survival*, *The Limits to Growth*, and *Small is Beautiful*, Britain had a Conservative government which was basically unsympathetic to the 'anti-growth' argument. In 1974, there was a change of government. The new Labour Secretary of State for the Environment was Anthony Crosland, who was equally unsympathetic. More than any other prominent British politician, he had argued in detail the case for believing that economic growth could bring social as well as purely economic benefits, largely because it made possible increases in expenditure on public services without the need to introduce politically unpopular increases in tax rates to pay for them.

In 1971, the Fabian Society published a pamphlet, *A Social Democratic Britain*, in which he replied to 'parts of the conservationist lobby'.

> Their approach is hostile to growth in principle and indifferent to the needs of ordinary people. It has a manifest class bias, and reflects a set of middle and upper class value judgements. Its champions are often kindly and dedicated people. But they are affluent and fundamentally, though of course not consciously, they want to kick the ladder down behind them. They are highly selective in their concern, being militant mainly about threats to rural peace and wildlife and well loved beauty spots; they are little concerned with the far more desperate problem of the urban environment in which 80 per cent of our fellow citizens live.[17]

6

My working class constituents have their own version of
the environment, which is equally valid and which calls for
economic growth. They want lower housing densities and
better schools and hospitals. They want washing machines
and refrigerators to relieve domestic drudgery. They want
cars, and the freedom they give on weekends and holidays.
And they want package tour holidays to Majorca, even if
this means more noise of night flights and eating fish and
chips on previously secluded beaches – and why should
they too not enjoy the sun? And they want these things not
. . . because their minds have been brain-washed and their
tastes contrived by advertising, but because the things are
desirable in themselves. . . .

In fact the anti-growth approach is not only unacceptable
in terms of values; it is absurd in terms of the environment
itself. . . . For the greater part of the environmental problem stems not from present or future growth, but from
past growth. It is largely a backlog problem – the legacy of
100 years of unplanned growth. It is a problem of *existing*
slum housing, polluted rivers, derelict land and belching
factories. Even if we stopped all further growth tomorrow
we should still need to spend huge additional sums on
coping with pollution; it will, for example, cost hundreds
of millions of pounds to clear our rivers of their present
pollution. . . . We have no chance of finding these huge
sums from a near-static GNP, any more than we could
find the extra sums we want for health or education or
any of our other goals. Only rapid growth will give us
any possibility.[18]

In saying this, Crosland was articulating the general view of
most politicians. Considerations of justice for working-class
people were further reinforced by the need to win their votes,
and those of better-off people who also wanted higher material
living standards. No politician trying to get elected has ever
found it easy to embrace the anti-growth cause.

In Defence of Economic Growth

Wilfred Beckerman's *In Defence of Economic Growth* (1974)
was, according to his publishers, 'the first reasoned and fully

7

documented defence of economic growth'.[19] Dr Beckerman is
an economist who was a member of the UK Royal Commission
on Environmental Pollution from 1970 to 1973.

In some respects his book echoes Crosland in speaking up
for working-class people who want holidays abroad and more
and better consumer durables, and in attacking the middle-class
bias of the anti-growth movement. This theme links the debate
about growth in the 1970s back to debates about 'affluence' in
the 1950s and 1960s.

He also specifically criticizes *The Limits to Growth*. 'But, of
course, if every past trend were projected to continue exponentially into the future, one could arrive at any sort of absurd
conclusion one liked.'[20] In fact, he argues, human societies react
to dangerous trends and try to do something about them. There
is no inevitability about disaster – and the evidence is that
dangerous trends are already being moderated and corrected
in a variety of ways.

Some of these ways are ones which economists generally are
very familiar with. Scarcity of a resource tends to make it more
expensive, which slows down the rate at which it is used up, and
stimulates the search for greater quantities of the resource, for
substitutes for it, and for technologies that can do without it or
use less of it. It also makes recycling more profitable. In all these
ways, the operations of the market tend naturally to combat
any tendency for natural resource stocks to become exhausted.
Society could make further use of the price mechanism through
government action to impose taxes on products or processes
which cause pollution.

Looking at the history of the past 100 years or so, it is clear,
according to Beckerman, that economic growth in Britain has
been accompanied by improvements in the urban environment
and the general health of the population, an increase in leisure
time, and a reduction in air and water pollution.

The extreme answers of the anti-growth lobby are not only
dangerous but unnecessary: changes in legislation and technology, together with the operation of the price mechanism, will
basically be sufficient to deal with the problems. Referring to
the anti-materialism argument put forward by Schumacher and
others, Beckerman says: 'The notion that mankind can now be
made to abandon his age-old continual rise in aspirations and
needs and to accept the self-denying rejection of goods and

services that has been preached for thousands of years by the inspired leaders of great religions, without any effect on the vast mass of the population, is unrealistic.'[21] 'Only an altogether unparalleled optimism can lead one to believe that the vast mass of the population will voluntarily accept an abandonment of the goal of economic growth, at least for the foreseeable future. This means that if growth were to be abandoned as an objective of policy, democracy too would have to be abandoned.'[22]

Mounting Greenery

Though not a major influence on the debate, *Mounting Greenery* (1989) is useful both because it is up to date at the time of writing this book, and because it is broadly representative of the response of the free market Right to these issues. *Mounting Greenery* is an Institute of Economic Affairs pamphlet written by Robert Whelan.

Many of the economic arguments he puts forward are the same as Beckerman's, but there is less emphasis on the need for government intervention, and a generally more optimistic and triumphant tone. 'The same ingenuity which has given us the most rapid pace of scientific advance in the history of humanity will also give us the answer to any problems which our activities create.'[23] 'Market forces and human ingenuity will always take care of shortages by providing solutions which leave us better off than we were before.'[24]

The pamphlet sets out to examine the 'extraordinary phenomenon' of green politics. According to Whelan, 'The Greens predict the end of the world *as a result of men and women going about their ordinary business*' (his emphasis). There can surely be no more disturbing idea for a conservatively-minded person than that there is something so dangerously wrong with 'ordinary business'. 'The Greens have persuaded people that human activities, and particularly the lifestyles of Western consumerist societies, are not just damaging or immoral; they will lead to the end of life on earth, at least in its present form, in the near future.'[25] The Greens 'are already demanding the implementation of policies which would have a serious effect on the material standard of living in both the developed and the developing world. . . .' 'However, before we start dismantling the engine of industrialism which has given the Western nations

9

the highest standard of living the world has ever known, and which promises the same degree of progress for the less developed nations, we do at least have the right to ask, *Are you sure?*'[26]

The pamphlet then discusses some major environmental issues and draws attention to conflicting estimates (e.g. of the rate of deforestation), uncertainty (e.g. about the greenhouse effect), and lack of data (for example, about species loss). He argues that the state of the evidence does not justify paying the costs involved in ending economic growth. In the case of depletion of the ozone layer, he does appear to accept that the evidence justifies action, and says that appropriate action is already being taken. This 'demonstrates that we have the capacity to respond to environmental threats, however serious these may be'.[27]

Whelan argues that the increasing prosperity which growth brings helps to solve environmental problems:

> Prosperous societies like the Western democracies are clean, healthy and pleasant to live in because we generate enough wealth to pay for our basic needs, and still have enough left over to pay for environmental projects which make life more pleasant.
>
> Poor countries, like many of those in the Soviet bloc and sub-Saharan Africa, are comparatively dirty, degraded and unhealthy because where people are scraping for a living they do not have time to worry about preserving the environment.[28]

Since green policies would produce poverty worldwide, all countries would then lack the resources to deal with environmental problems.

Whilst rejecting the green emphasis on the environmental costs of growth, Whelan accepts the view of Schumacher and others that there have been high psychological and spiritual costs to the direction taken by Western societies. For Whelan, these provide part of the explanation for the 'rise of Greenery':

> We have achieved the highest standard of living and the most rapid rate of technological progress ever known, but somewhere along the way the spiritual dimension of human nature has been neglected. With the decline in influence of the churches and the virtual abandonment

10

by most schools of the teaching of religion, many people now grow up without any idea of why they are here or what they are supposed to be doing. Into this spiritual vacuum comes . . . Greenery, offering people a clearly defined world view, in which they can participate in the salvation or destruction of the planet by riding a bicycle or using hairspray.[29]

But 'the spiritual values out of which the movement has grown are essentially pagan rather than Christian. People who are genuinely looking for an answer to life's most fundamental questions have turned away from the light of revealed religion to the darkness of the forests'.[29]

As this pamphlet makes clear, the debate about growth is no ordinary argument within economics. It ranges from scientific issues such as whether there is adequate statistical evidence for the existence of the greenhouse effect to archetypal clashes between light and darkness, 'materialism' and 'spirituality'. Almost twenty years after *The Limits to Growth*, the debate continues. What has changed about it in recent years, however, is the increasing influence of people arguing for some sort of compromise or synthesis. Two examples of this are referred to in the next section.

A SUSTAINABLE COMPROMISE?

The Brundtland Report

Our Common Future, usually referred to as the Brundtland Report, is the report of the World Commission on Environment and Development, set up by the United Nations and chaired by Gro Harlem Brundtland, ex-Prime Minister of Norway. It was published in 1987. Mrs Brundtland says in the foreword that she sees the report as a sequel to the Brandt Report on North–South issues and the Palme Report on disarmament.

The outlook of *Our Common Future* has much in common with that of the Brandt Report. Brundtland places environmental issues within the context of Third World poverty and development. 'It is impossible to separate economic development issues from environment issues; many forms of development erode the environmental resources upon which they must be based, and environmental degradation can undermine economic development. Poverty is a major cause and effect of global environmental problems. It is therefore futile to attempt to deal with environmental problems without a broader perspective that encompasses the factors underlying world poverty and international inequality.'[30]

Although the Report does not accept that the problems the world faces are caused by economic growth, it does agree with the anti-growth lobby that these problems are extremely serious, urgent, and large-scale:

Over the course of this century, the relationship between the human world and the planet that sustains it has undergone a profound change. When the century began, neither human numbers nor technology had the power to radically alter planetary systems. As the century closes, not only do vastly increased human numbers and their activities have that power, but major, unintended changes are occurring in the atmosphere, in soils, in waters, among plants and animals, and in the relations among all of these.[31]

Brundtland is not against growth *per se*, only against some particular forms of growth. 'What is needed now is a new era of economic growth – growth that is . . . socially and environmentally sustainable.'[32] The key phrase in the Brundtland Report is 'sustainable development': 'Sustainable development is development that meets the needs of the present without compromising the ability of future generations to meet their own needs . . . sustainability implies a concern for social equity between generations, a concern that must logically be extended to equity within each generation.'[33] The Report sets out policy recommendations which its authors believe would enable industry, agriculture, and energy to be developed on a sustainable basis, for example through greater conservation, recycling, and efficiency in the use of energy and other resources.

The Report is a compromise document, both in the sense that it was written by a committee which was divided on some key issues, such as nuclear power, and also in the sense that it elaborates a compromise position in the debate between the advocates of continued growth and the advocates of non-growth. Like most compromises, 'sustainable development' is viewed with suspicion by both sides. For the pro-growth side of the argument, 'sustainable development' is dangerous because it may mean in practice no growth and development at all. For the anti-growth side, the 'development' part carries the danger that growth will take priority, with 'sustainable' becoming merely an after-thought, or a slogan which doesn't represent a thought at all.

The *Blueprint for a Green Economy* (1989), known as the Pearce Report, starts from Brundtland's concept of 'sustainable development' and attempts to make it more precise, particularly in the context of the UK. The Report was commissioned by the UK Department of the Environment. Some issues referred to in the Pearce Report particularly relevant to the topic of economic indicators will be discussed in chapter 4 of this book. Pearce basically endorses what I am calling 'the Brundtland compromise', rejecting the idea that economic growth is inherently and necessarily bad or unsustainable.[34]

BEYOND THE GROWTH DEBATE

The debate about economic growth has been an extremely productive one, with a number of important offshoots. It has been a major stimulus to the development of green politics. Many Green parties take as their main starting-point opposition to continued economic growth. For example, the English Green Party's 'Philosophical Basis' says on its first page: 'The relentless pursuit of economic growth, accompanied by rising material expectations within an ever increasing world population, has brought humankind to the brink of a disaster which is unprecedented in history. . . . From henceforward the main political battles will not be between Left and Right in the traditional sense, but between the supporters of a steady state economy and growth.'[35] A detailed critique of *The Limits to Growth* study, *Thinking About The Future*, was published in 1973, and this has been followed by a whole literature on computer models of the world as a system, and a debate about projecting and predicting future environmental, economic, and other trends.[36] The growth debate has also helped to stimulate the development of 'New Economics', which this book is part of. New Economics aims to bring into economic debate the environmental and human factors so often left out by mainstream economic theory.[37]

The growth debate itself has been an unsatisfactory one, because the 'growth' which the 'anti-growthists' have attacked has not usually been the same thing as the 'growth' which the 'pro-growthists' have rushed to defend. This is mainly because the chief influence on the thinking of the anti-growthists has been ecology, whilst the main influence on the defenders of growth has been economics.

In economics, 'economic growth' is *defined as* an increase in gross national product or gross domestic product (GDP). The figure for the rate of growth leaves unanswered a whole series of questions about the composition of output between industry, agriculture, services, etc.; between polluting and non-polluting sectors; between resource depleting and conserving activities; and so on. The GNP total and its rate of growth are seen by economists as important figures, but what they can tell us is strictly limited.

In ecology, the paradigm case of growth is growth in the population of a species. The normal pattern is that populations grow until some feature of their environment, perhaps a predator or a limited food supply, brings that growth to a halt, or pushes it into reverse. The anti-growthists imagine that economic growth is a similar process. But clearly the size of the human population doesn't by itself determine the degree of environmental impact, because human beings consume different goods and services, use different technologies to produce them, and are organized in different sorts of societies. The hope is (for example, in *A Blueprint for Survival*) that if the population is multiplied by GDP per head, then that will give a reliable indication of environmental impact.[38]

Since population multiplied by GDP per head equals total GDP, GDP growth is seen as an indicator of growth in environmental impact. Although anti-growth ecologists use GDP figures for this purpose, when their arguments are examined more closely, it becomes clear that GDP growth is not what really interests them. What they are concerned with primarily is growth in environmental impact – pollution, extinction of species, deforestation, rate of consumption of energy and materials – and in the processes which produce it. The *Blueprint* simply says that GDP 'appears to provide the most convenient measure of ecological demand', and it is ecological demand which is the prime concern.[38] *The Limits to Growth* talks about 'economic growth' but in its equations it is careful to use growth in industrial output rather than growth in GDP. Schumacher talks about 'growth', but again it is not specifically GDP or GNP growth which interest him.[39]

The problem about this is that GDP and GNP are not, in fact, accurate indicators of total environmental impact or 'ecological demand'. Growth in GDP can be growth in the output of very different sorts of things, with very different environmental impacts. It seems to me that the anti-growthists would make their case much more convincing if they used indicators which actually measure damage to the environment, in place of GDP, which doesn't. One of the aims of this book is to suggest and argue for some indicators they might use – in order to identify the variables which really do need to be levelled off or reversed in direction.

The green movement needs to be clearer now in its objectives and analysis than it was at the time of the *Blueprint* and *The Limits to Growth* because now it is listened to far more, and in some parts of the world has a share in government. It sounded a warning by talking vaguely about 'growth', but if it is to generate appropriate constructive policies, it will need to look further into the issues. This book is intended as a contribution to that process, looking first into GDP and the accounting system it is based on, national income accounting, and then into other indicators which can measure what is happening to the environment and to human beings.

2

THE ORIGINS OF
NATIONAL INCOME
ACCOUNTING

Gross national product and gross domestic product are totals produced by a set of procedures known as 'national income accounting'. Some of the problems which arise from these procedures are discussed in chapter 3. In this chapter, I shall look at the context in which the current national income accounting methods were first worked out. Measures of total national income such as GNP and GDP have become such a familiar and widely accepted part of economics that it is easy to forget the fact that they were invented at specific times for specific purposes.

There is a long history of attempts to estimate total national income, from Sir William Petty's estimates for England in the seventeenth century, through to the present day. Petty says in his book, *Political Arithmetick* (1690): 'Instead of using only comparative and superlative Words . . . I have taken the course . . . to express myself in Terms of Number, Weight, or Measure.'[1] He tried to establish some statistical basis for the discussion of economic issues.

The major breakthroughs to national income accounting in its present detailed form were made in the context of wartime planning, in the USA and UK particularly, and in response to the depression of the 1930s. According to Don Patinkin (*Anticipations of the General Theory?*), 'we can regard the statistical revolution which brought about the introduction of official national income estimates in both the US and Britain as an example of a technological improvement stimulated by war; except that in the US it was World War I which (with some time lag) fulfilled this function, whereas Britain for some reason had to wait for World War II'.[2] One of the reasons for regarding this as a 'statistical revolution' is that 'these estimates no longer resulted from the sporadic research activities of individual scholars using different methods which they respectively applied to different, isolated years, but from the organised activity of official government agencies which systematically produced current annual estimates on as homogeneous a basis as possible'.[3]

In the 1920s and early 1930s, national income accounting was seen by its advocates as primarily a matter of being simply more efficient and systematic about collecting statistical information. National income accounting was given a greater theoretical significance by John Maynard Keynes. In his *General Theory* (1936), he ascribed a key role to 'aggregate real income', also referred to 'the national income (or national dividend)',[4] and complained about the inadequacy of UK statistics of total income and investment.[5] Many of the economic statistics collected by governments in the post-war period have been designed essentially to produce figures to put into the equations set out in, or which have been derived from, the *General Theory*. The central variable in these equations is 'Y' (national income), and so the calculation of figures for national income is essential for any attempt to manage the economy on Keynesian principles.

Keynes also played an important role in the development of national income accounting for wartime planning. He argued for such accounting in the course of writing about how British government expenditure on the Second World War could be financed. It was clearly necessary to have reliable figures for total taxable income, in order to derive estimates of potential government revenue. In an article in *The Economic Journal* (December 1939), Keynes wrote: 'The statistics on which to base an estimate of the income potential of the country and of the proportion of it which can be made available to the Government are very inadequate.'[6] In 'Paying for the War' (two influential articles published in *The Times* in November 1939 and published in a revised form as *How to Pay for the War*) Keynes makes a similar point, and sets out rough estimates for the figures he would like to see worked on in a more thorough way. Keynes followed this up by writing notes and letters criticizing the 1940 Budget and putting forward proposals for the 1941 Budget.

As a result, he was invited to take part within government in work on the 1941 Budget, the first to be based on a national income accounting analytical framework. On the same day as the Budget, a White Paper was published, setting out the national income and expenditure statistics on which the Budget decisions were based. Keynes described this as 'a revolution in public finance'.[7]

Present-day national income accounting is therefore the result of a combination of the practical need to gather reliable information in wartime with the theoretical framework provided by Keynesian economics. It has been shaped by the two main concerns of economists during the period in which it was created: government finance and unemployment. Problems have arisen in recent years from attempts to apply it in other contexts and for other purposes.

The role of national income

National income measurements such as GNP and GDP were not intended by those who devised them to be measures of total welfare or total environmental impact. Yet in the debate about economic growth, as we have seen in the previous chapter, they have been used in both of these roles. Defenders of economic growth usually see average GDP per person – i.e. GDP divided by the population of a country – as giving some indication of the standard of living or level of economic welfare in that country. The anti-growthists often use GDP as an indicator of the rate of environmental destruction (or 'ecological demand').

The use of GDP and GNP as measures of economic welfare can be traced back historically, not through attempts to estimate figures for total national income, but through debates about 'value'. Eighteenth- and nineteenth-century discussions of economic issues often centred around attempts to discover the nature of 'value' and where it comes from. Economists who wanted to measure value in quantitative – and hence, as they saw it, precise – terms were attracted by the apparent simplicity of using money as a measure of value. Because prices indicate how much money people are willing to pay for a product, prices came to be widely seen as measuring the usefulness or utility of the goods and services bought. A higher price meant that something had more utility, and hence was more valuable. *If* this is true of individual goods and services, then there is some basis for using aggregate measures such as total expenditure (one of the ways of calculating GDP) as measures of the total utility or value generated by the economy as a whole.

GNP and GDP today play an ambiguous role: on the one hand, they are seen as purely objective financial measures, providing some information about flows of money through the economy; on the other hand, they simultaneously play the very different role of being used – primarily by politicians rather than economists – as measurements of the overall success and progress of an economy, the value it has generated, and the human happiness or welfare derived from it. In its first role, as a measure of flows of money, GDP and GNP have a lot of validity; but in their second role, as a measure of total value (or welfare, or progress), they are much more problematic. Some of the problems involved will be discussed in the next chapter.

Some definitions

Before looking at the problems of national income accounting, it may be useful at this point to define briefly some relevant terms:

Gross domestic product (GDP) is the total value in money terms of all the production in a country in one year. It is measured in three different ways (which should all end up with the same total): through adding the value of the goods and services produced, through adding the expenditure on them, and through adding the incomes received from producing them. Production where no money changes hands – such as unpaid domestic work – is therefore excluded from GDP. Money changing hands where there is no production – such as gifts – is also excluded.

Gross national product (GNP) is GDP plus rents, interest, profits, and dividends flowing into a country from abroad, minus rents, interest, profits, and dividends paid out to people in other countries. GNP therefore measures the total income received by the inhabitants of a country. GNP depends on where the owners are located; GDP depends on where the economic activity is located. In a country with a lot of foreign investment in it but very little investment by its inhabitants in other countries, there will be a net outflow of 'property income' (rents, interest, profits, and dividends). This will result in a GNP much lower than its GDP.

GDP or GNP per capita, i.e. per head or per person, is GDP or GNP divided by the total population of the country. This gives a figure often described as measuring the 'average standard of living'.

Net national product (NNP) is GNP minus capital depreciation. Some of the money spent in a country in a year – and therefore included in GNP – is expenditure simply to replace machinery and factory and office buildings which have worn out. In that sense, it isn't 'new' expenditure. It is excluded from NNP by subtracting it from the GNP figure.

National income accounting is the accounting activities, carried out according to various rules (e.g. to avoid counting the same production twice over in the course of arriving at a particular total), which generates figures for GDP, GNP, NNP, and their component parts.

3

PROBLEMS OF NATIONAL INCOME ACCOUNTING

The previous chapter referred to two roles played by GNP: a strictly economic role, in which GNP is used as a measure of flows of money in an economy; and a more political role, in which GNP is seen as a measure of the 'welfare', 'value', 'success', or 'progress' made by an economy. In addition, the anti-growth arguments of the authors of *A Blueprint for Survival* and others have given GNP a third role: they have used it as a measurement of the pressure which the economy puts on the environment.

This chapter is concerned with the second role, in which GNP is used to measure 'how well the economy is doing'. Economists often claim that they do not use GNP and GNP growth to evaluate economies, and it is true that many are careful to stick to 'the growth rate has increased' as opposed to 'the growth rate has improved' or 'the growth rate has increased, therefore things must be getting better'. Yet repeatedly, the language of automatic evaluation creeps into talk about GNP (the higher, the better) and growth (the faster, the better). This is especially the case when discussion of GNP comes out of specialist economics and into public debate – in the newspapers, in politicians' speeches, on television.

In this chapter, I will put forward a number of reasons for believing that GNP going up is not necessarily a good thing, and that growth increasing does not necessarily represent an improvement either. In other words, it will be argued that GNP is not a good indicator of welfare. There are two main stages to the argument. First, I will argue that GNP is not even a good measurement of total output of goods and services, because it measures only those which are paid for. Second, I will then argue that changes in the output of goods and services, and changes in the level of welfare (or well-being, or total utility), do not necessarily coincide.

PROBLEMS OF INCOME AND OUTPUT

One of the ways in which national income accounting measures output is by measuring income. Only when output of goods and services is matched by a flow of money – someone's expenditure becoming someone's income – is that output included in the GNP. Yet there are also important categories of output not matched by money flows.

Problem 1: unpaid domestic labour

The biggest category of output not reflected in measurements of income is unpaid domestic labour, principally housework, childcare and, in many countries, agricultural work. One result of this is that the official statistics systematically understate the contribution made by women to total output.[1]

If someone eats out, part of what is paid for the meal is a payment to someone else for the work of doing the cooking. This is included in the GNP. If, however, instead of eating out, I do the cooking myself, then despite the fact that exactly the same work is involved, this counts for nothing in the GNP statistics because the work has been carried out 'within the household', and no money has changed hands. Similarly, if instead of looking after a baby at home, I start paying someone else to, the GNP is thereby increased, even though essentially the same activity is happening as was happening before.

As well as resulting in an under-representation of women's work in the national accounts, this feature of GNP also tends to overstate the rate of growth which takes place during industrialization. For example, in discussing the history of economic growth in Britain during the industrial revolution, the historian A. J. Taylor drew attention to 'activities like brewing, baking, market-gardening and dressmaking which in the pre-industrial era had largely been undertaken as domestic pursuits but which in the nineteenth century became increasingly institutionalized.

In the former state they escape and in the latter gain inclusion in the national income estimates; and to this extent there is a bias in favour of growth in the later figures.'[2] Current switches from domestic to non-domestic production in industrializing Third World countries create the same bias in calculations of growth rates.

Problem 2: non-money transactions outside the household

Similar problems arise from output outside the household not matched by flows of money. An example of this is barter. If the process of industrialization reduces the proportion of economic transactions which are carried out through barter – as appears to be the case historically – then the switch from barter to money will show up in the national accounts as a tendency for GNP to rise, thus overstating the rate of economic growth.

Similarly, people doing favours for friends, relatives and neighbours is excluded from the accounts if no money changes hands. Unpaid charity work and activity in voluntary organizations is also excluded. Because these forms of activity do not count in national income accounting, there is a tendency to ignore or devalue their significance whenever GNP is used as a measure of overall welfare or progress.

There is, of course, a separate problem that even where money does change hands it may go unrecorded, often in order to evade taxation. Though this is a practical problem for the compilers of national income accounts, there is not really any conceptual problem here, simply a need to improve techniques of estimation.

PROBLEMS OF OUTPUT AND WELFARE

Even in the case of those parts of output which are matched by flows of money, there are problems about the relationship between output and welfare. This set of problems can be divided into a number of categories: problems of averaging and comparisons; problems of stock and depreciation; problems about other sources of welfare, and problems about inefficiency in providing welfare.

23

PROBLEMS OF AVERAGING AND COMPARISONS

Problem 3: distribution of income

In a country with an equal distribution of income, an average figure for national income per head gives a realistic reflection of each person's income. But in a country with a very unequal distribution, a concentration of income in a small minority of the population will result in the majority of people in that country being well below the figure for average income.

Average and total national figures must obviously ignore the 'details' of how the total is distributed between different sections of the population. But if total GNP, or GNP per head, or their growth rates, are to be used to measure the desirability or otherwise of particular societies or government policies, they should be used in conjunction with measures of such 'details' as distribution of income. Otherwise, they will prove highly misleading as measurements of living standards.

Problem 4: differences in needs and circumstances

National income accounting measures the production of goods and services. However, many goods and services are only necessary in certain circumstances. For example, if I live in a cold country, I will need heaters which would be unnecessary in a warm climate. If I live in a village, I may buy a car to travel into the town centre, but if I live in the town, I may walk instead. Differences in circumstances will create different needs for goods and services: someone living in the middle of Iceland would have to spend a lot on heating and on travelling to the nearest shops, without as a result being warmer or more able to buy things than most people in Italy spending far less.

Similarly, if the population rises in a particular year because a lot of babies are born that year, that has different implications for consumption and living standards from an increase in population due to a tendency for old people to live longer. The consumption needs of an old person may, for example, be twice that of a baby. In order to arrive at a figure for GNP per person which is valid for making comparisons (between different years, different countries, etc.), perhaps the population figures should

24

be weighted, so that an old person is counted as equivalent to two babies.

As soon as we move away from the simple rule that it is sheer numbers of people which matter, and start to distinguish between different types of people, in different circumstances and with different needs, then there is no end to the statistical difficulties this can cause. It is easier, therefore, for statisticians to make the assumption that differences in the consumption needs of different people are best ignored. But ignoring them does not mean that they will go away or cease to be significant.

Problem 5: the use of exchange rates in international comparisons

International comparisons of GNP and GNP per head depend on rates of conversion from the currency of one country to the currency of another. If current market exchange rates are used for this purpose, then the comparisons made are as unstable as the exchange rates. A fall in the exchange rate of a currency automatically produces a reduction, by the same percentage, in the figures for the living standards of the country in comparison to other countries. Fluctuations in exchange rates produce fluctuations in comparative GNP statistics which may, at for example a 3 per cent reduction in the exchange rate during a particular day, be sufficient to wipe out statistically in that one day the gains achieved by economic growth in a whole year.

A related difficulty with the use of current market exchange rates is that it ignores the possibility that a particular currency may be 'overvalued' or 'undervalued'. International comparisons of GNP on this basis therefore tend to reflect government policies to influence the exchange rate up or down (e.g. by adjusting interest rates) as much as they do 'real' differences in the value of output or income.

PROBLEMS OF STOCKS AND DEPRECIATION

People derive benefits from both stocks and flows, whereas GNP measures only flows. This gives rise to a number of problems.

Problem 6: wealth and depreciation

GNP measures total income, and therefore reflects the benefits which people derive from having an income. But it does not measure the value of people's existing possessions, and therefore does not reflect the benefits people derive from them.

An exception is made in the case of housing, where an estimate is made and included in GNP for the value derived from owning a house. This is 'imputed rent', which is the rent which it is estimated that owner-occupiers would be charging and paying themselves if they weren't owner-occupiers, but were two different people, landlord and tenant.

This same procedure might be applied to other possessions, e.g. imputed values from owning a car, a cooker, or a washing machine. This would turn GNP into a more accurate measurement of living standards. If this is not done, then GNP will continue failing to take into account not only the benefits people derive from what they own, but also the depreciation of their possessions. At present, nothing is subtracted from GNP if a car, a cooker, or a washing machine breaks down and is thrown away. In fact, there is instead a tendency for GNP to rise, because people generally want to replace what they have lost, and so new goods may be produced, all of them adding to the GNP figures. An economy with a rapid 'throughput' of resources and goods will have a high GNP but without achieving a high level of ownership of goods at any time.

Problem 7: 'environmental wealth' and its depreciation

National income accounting records the use of resources when they are paid for. But when they are free, no money changes hands, and therefore nothing is recorded in the national accounts. A great many natural resources and 'services' provided by the environment in fact *are* free. If the air takes away smoke which I have created, and I don't have to pay for using the air, then I am getting a benefit from 'environmental wealth', and that benefit will not be reflected in the GNP figures. If the effect of the smoke I create is to reduce the quality of the air, and therefore to reduce the benefits which other people derive from it, that cost – an example of 'environmental depreciation' – will not be reflected in the GNP figures either.

A great deal of economic activity is concerned with turning environmental wealth into current income and output. If coal or oil is extracted from the earth, GNP counts their money value, but nothing is subtracted from GNP to reflect the fact that the stock of coal or oil has been reduced. If a forest is cut down, the value of the timber is counted in the GNP, but no account is taken of the benefits which were derived from the existence of the forest, such as absorption of carbon dioxide (unless these benefits were paid for) or of the loss of these benefits when the forest is destroyed.

Difficult choices are constantly being made between the conservation of the environment and natural resources, and their use in ways which destroy them. National income accounting, where it is used for evaluative purposes, favours the use and destruction of resources because money is more likely to change hands for this, rather than leaving them alone, where money doesn't usually change hands.

Not only are the benefits from the environment, and the costs of its destruction, not counted, but also the expenditure necessary to repair damage and compensate for costs *is* counted. Thus GNP can rise twice over from environmental destruction. For example, if a factory pollutes a river in the course of producing something, the money value of what was produced is included in GNP, and *then* if the river is cleaned up, the money paid for the cleaning up is also included in GNP, whereas this expenditure was necessary simply to return the river to the state it was in before. It doesn't represent the creation of any new wealth or welfare.

Problem 8: human beings – and their 'depreciation'

A third form of 'stock' from which people derive benefits – along with stocks of possessions and stocks of natural resources and other 'environmental wealth' – is stocks of 'human capital', i.e. people seen in their role as resources able to contribute to output. A person's value as 'human capital' depends on the education and training they have received, their state of health, and initially on reproduction and childcare. All of these therefore contribute to the economy as forms of 'human investment', just as buying and servicing machinery contributes.

'Human capital' can depreciate, just as machinery does. Work in unhealthy conditions 'depreciates human capital'. Apart from the cost to the individual, unhealthy people are not able to work as efficiently as healthy people. Work which is monotonous, degrading, or overspecialized, may also 'depreciate' people.

National income accounting is concerned with the depreciation of machinery, which is subtracted from gross national product to arrive at net national product. Depreciation to human beings, on the other hand, is not reflected in NNP or anywhere else in the national income accounting system – except perhaps as a tendency for GNP to rise because of expenditure to reverse the depreciation (such as hospital operations).

Problem 9: positional goods

One way in which depreciation can take place is through increases in the production of 'positional goods'. These are goods which derive their value from the fact that not everyone has them. For example, if I have a ticket which entitles me to sit on a private beach when very few other people are allowed in, the value of the ticket will decline if more are printed, more and more people obtain the additional tickets, and the place becomes more crowded. The more tickets printed, the lower the value of the ones which people already own. When I paid for my ticket, its money value was counted in GNP. When my ticket declined in value because an extra thousand of them were sold, the 'depreciation' wasn't subtracted from GNP.

Significant examples of this include: cars, whose value to their owner tends to fall whenever new cars are added to the road space available; houses, whose value to their occupier tends to fall if extra houses are built nearby; and status symbols, which fall in value if more people possess them. A growing economy with a high proportion of positional goods is not necessarily growing in total welfare.[3]

PROBLEMS OF OTHER SOURCES OF WELFARE

A further set of reasons why total output does not give an accurate measure of welfare derives from the sources of welfare other than output and stocks. These include some sources which national income measures have little or no bearing on, such as peace of mind, happiness in personal relationships, etc. There are two other sources which do, however, have some connection with national income accounting: leisure time and the quality of life at work.

Problem 10: leisure time

National income accounting distinguishes sharply between the two ways in which increased productivity can be used. Where increases in productivity and efficiency are used to produce more goods, GNP records 'economic growth'. Where the same increases in productivity are used to produce the same goods as before but in less time, reducing working hours and increasing time available for leisure, GNP ignores the change. The aim of raising economic growth therefore biases discussions about policy towards taking the first choice (extra production) rather than the second (more leisure), even though opting for more leisure may be a perfectly legitimate and sensible choice to make.

Problem 11: the quality of life at work

The model of the economy implicit in national income accounting sees welfare as derived from output, and output as derived from economic activity, of which work is a major component. But welfare may also be derived directly from work. In other words, people may enjoy their work.

If there were no such non-money benefits, incomes would presumably have to be higher than at present if people were to be persuaded to continue doing the same paid work. If people were paid more, GNP would rise. Yet welfare would remain the same, because the rise in GNP would simply represent the compensation necessary to counteract the loss in non-money sources of welfare.

Changes in the quality of life in paid work may also either improve or depreciate 'human capital'. This was discussed in problem 8.

PROBLEMS OF INEFFICIENCY IN PROVIDING WELFARE

Where welfare is derived from goods and services, the money

value of these goods and services is often a poor indication of the amount of welfare derived, for a variety of reasons.

Problem 12: inefficient private provision

If the public water supply fails to work, and people go out to supermarkets and buy bottled mineral water instead, GNP will register an increase, because a pint of bottled water costs far more than a pint of water from a tap. Similarly, if public transport services are cut back, and people buy cars to make the same journeys, GNP will register an increase, because more expense is involved. Part of that extra expense may represent an improvement in welfare (travelling by car may be better than travelling by bus), but part of it is simply a result of people's range of choices being reduced. The more expensive option becomes the only one possible. When people choose it, GNP rises. If the cheaper option becomes available again and some people choose that, GNP will fall.

If public policy aims at increasing GNP, therefore, there will be a built-in bias in favour of more expensive ways of providing services, and against cheaper, and in that sense more efficient, ways.

Problem 13: 'inefficiency' in consumer decisions

Another source of inefficiency in the link between output and welfare derives from the ways people make decisions about what to buy. People may choose goods which bring short-term benefits but long-term costs, for instance to their health. People may choose goods they would not have chosen if they had had better information about the range of options available, and they may be misled by advertisers' and manufacturers' claims. People in governments may choose to spend public money on goods which bring few benefits.

Problem 14: 'inefficiency' in production

GNP values output according to the amount of money spent on it. Something which is expensive to produce is likely to be expensive to buy, and therefore to contribute more to GNP than a cheap product. With technological change, goods often become cheaper to produce and cheaper to buy. There is then a tendency for GNP to fall, even though consumers are clearly better off than they were before.

Problem 15: the valuation of output reflects the distribution of income

Prices of products are influenced not only by the costs of producing them but also by what customers are willing to pay. This in turn depends on how much money different customers have. How different goods and services are valued in national income accounting therefore depends partly on how purchasing power is distributed between different consumers. The products which richer people can afford to buy tend to be more expensive – not only because they can afford to buy them, but also because producers can get away with charging a lot for them. The result is that such products count for a lot in the GNP figures.

Problem 16: the diminishing marginal utility of money

People with very low incomes can afford to spend money only on their highest priorities. If incomes rise, it becomes possible to move down the lists of priorities. If this is true for a whole country, then if average GNP per head rises, the additional goods and services bought represent lower priorities than the goods and services which were bought before. A country whose GNP per head doubles is therefore unlikely to double in welfare, because its initial GNP per head included a high proportion of necessities, whereas its new double-level GNP per head includes a high proportion of goods and services which could easily be dispensed with without any significant loss to people. GNP per head economic growth rates therefore systematically overstate the rate of growth in welfare.

CONCLUSION

The procedures of national income accounting introduce a series of biases into any process of decision-making which has increasing GNP as one of its objectives. For example, there is a bias in favour of the production of new goods and the depletion of resources, and against durability and conservation; in favour of using technological advance to boost production and against using it to reduce working time; in favour of the production of expensive luxuries, and the redirection of the resources to make them away from cheaper products; etc.

However, the existence of all these problems and biases does not by itself make out the case for scrapping the use of GNP as an indicator of welfare, unless a better alternative, or set of alternatives, can be found. Many economists who acknowledge that there are difficulties with GNP and the accounting conventions it is based on, nevertheless argue that there is no alternative.

Having outlined some problems of existing national income accounting, the rest of this book will be concerned with trying to find a better alternative, either by modifying national income accounting in some way to create some form of 'adjusted national product', or through abandoning this framework and developing a different approach to measuring the economy.

4

POSSIBLE REFORMS IN NATIONAL INCOME ACCOUNTING

This chapter considers changes which could be made to national income accounting whilst retaining its existing basic framework. It may be possible to make additions, subtractions, and other changes to national income totals, to create some form of 'adjusted national product', 'measure of economic welfare', or 'welfare GNP'. Changes of this type might be based on any of the sixteen problems with national income accounting outlined in the previous chapter – or perhaps all of them simultaneously.

POSSIBLE ADDITIONS TO GNP

In response to problem 1 (outlined in the previous chapter), the problem of *unpaid domestic labour*, proposals have been made to add to GNP additional figures representing economic activity within the household. For example, it might be possible to add in estimates for the value in money terms of food preparation and cooking, cleaning, childcare, etc.

There are various difficulties with this proposal. Should these activities be valued according to the rate of pay which the person doing them would have earned in paid employment? The basis for doing so is that since the person concerned chose to do unpaid work within the household rather than paid employment, getting the unpaid work done must have been considered to be at least as valuable as the income which could have been gained in the same time through employment. There is therefore a 'revealed preference' which enables economists to take individuals' own estimates of the value of their unpaid work, and to use these in national income calculations.

What this would lead to, however, is the strange outcome that housework done by someone in a highly paid job is counted as more valuable than the same housework done by someone in a poorly paid job. Overall, one result of this would be counting housework done by men as generally more valuable than the same housework done by women.

Another way to value housework would be according to what would have to be paid for it if someone were to be employed to do it. Although this may be a better basis for assigning a value to housework, there is a further problem of deciding which activities within the household are to be included. Which unpaid activities count as 'unpaid work' (to be included in a reformed national income accounts) and which are 'leisure' (presumably still to be excluded, or perhaps valued as a positive benefit)? Can such a dividing line be drawn?

Though there is no perfect solution to this problem, it nevertheless seems likely that some way of including in GNP a figure for the value of economic activity internal to households would improve GNP as a measure of economic welfare in comparison to GNP as it is calculated at present, with non-money activity within households excluded. The possibility exists of constructing an adjusted national product on these lines.

This was called for by a United Nations conference held in Nairobi to complete the UN Decade for Women (1975–85), where government representatives agreed that women's unpaid work should be included in GNP, and also by a private member's bill introduced into the British House of Commons in 1989 by Mildred Gordon MP (the Counting Women's Unremunerated Work Bill).[1] Estimates for *non-money transactions outside the household* (problem 2) could be added on a similar basis.

Problems also arise from proposals to include the value of *leisure time* (problem 10) in an adjusted national product.[2] A value for this could be based on the average wage rate which people could have earned in the same time (thus implying the revealed preference that the leisure is worth at least as much per hour as the wage rate), but this has the effect of increasing the value of leisure time whenever, and to the extent that, the wage rate increases. Leisure also appears to decline in value if wages fall, and to be worth less to poorer people than to more highly paid people. And there are again the difficulties of drawing a line between leisure and 'productive' household activity.

However, time for leisure, including time to enjoy the consumption of goods and services bought, is clearly often as
valuable to people as the goods and services themselves, and
is in any case necessary for their use, and so once again there
is a case for including some figure for leisure in an adjusted
national product.

Thirdly, the *quality of life at work* (problem 11) could also be
taken into account, perhaps by estimating how much money
someone would need to be paid to give up various desirable
features of their working conditions or of the nature of their
work.

POSSIBLE SUBTRACTIONS FROM GNP

There are a variety of candidates for subtraction from GNP,
which generally tend to raise more difficult problems than
those arising from the possible additions. This is because the
problems with national income accounting which the possible
subtractions derive from are each based on concepts which
are extremely hard to make quantifiable. Concepts such as
'environmental depreciation' and 'positional goods' appear to
be fairly clear ideas in principle, but to assign a value to them in
money terms, in order to subtract what they refer to from GNP, is
very difficult. Here are some examples of the problems involved:

1 How can we put a money value on costs such as *accidents
   and dangers to health*? How much is a life worth, or the risk
   of loss of life? Various suggestions have been made, such as
   valuing someone's life as equivalent to their predicted future
   total income, or risks according to the insurance premiums
   people are willing to pay; but there is clearly something very
   unsatisfactory about these answers.
2 Although it may be desirable to deduct from GNP the value
   of *positional goods* (problem 9), few goods and services are
   completely positional. How can one quantify the proportion
   of the value of a good or service which represents its role as
   a positional good or service, and the proportion representing
   its role as directly useful in non-positional ways?
3 A variety of proposals have been made for deducting from
   GNP a figure for *'environmental depreciation'*.[3] In existing
   national income accounting, a distinction is made between

gross national product and net national product (NNP). NNP is what is left of GNP after the value of the depreciation of capital goods (such as machinery and factory and office buildings) has been subtracted. Depreciation is valued on the basis that a certain amount of expenditure on new capital goods is necessary to replace the goods which have worn out or declined in efficiency. This 'replacement investment' is held to give a figure for the money value of depreciation. Part of gross national product is investment, and part of this is replacement investment, which is subtracted from GNP to give net national product.

If we extend the concept of 'capital goods' to cover the 'natural capital' of mineral and other natural resources and the 'services' provided by the environment, then the concept of 'depreciation' can similarly be extended to cover the depletion of natural resources and the impairment of the capacity of the environment to provide its 'services' (such as the assimilation of waste and its capacity for renewing biological processes such as growing crops).

It then becomes possible to value depreciation as equivalent to the 'replacement investment' expenditure which would be necessary to get the environment and resources back to the state they were in at the beginning of the time-period being considered (usually the start of the year).

This is a useful idea which it is possible to develop. But there are some serious problems about it. One is that resource depletion and environmental destruction are often not reversible. There is therefore no possible level of expenditure sufficient to get the environment and resource base back to an earlier state. Where processes are reversible, the amount which has to be spent to reverse them may be extremely difficult to estimate because one may not know in advance whether a particular way of attempting to reverse them is going to be successful (e.g. attempting to reverse desertification). And if the environment only enters into our calculations because of the 'services' it provides to the economy, i.e. to human beings, then aspects of the environment which have no economic value to the human species are left out of consideration.

There is also the dangerous implication that any loss to the environment (unless we are willing to assign it a value of literally minus infinity pounds) can be compensated for by large enough increases in production, or by an improvement in some other aspect of the environment. Clearly the planet does not allow for that: it has many features which are each essential to the functioning of the world ecological system, and which therefore cannot be replaced or outweighed by substitute goods and services in the same sort of way as different consumer products like butter and margarine can be substituted for each other.

4 A similar extension of the concept of 'depreciation' could be made to cover damage done to *human capital*, i.e. people seen as providers of inputs to the production process, particularly labour. Similar problems arise with calculating this as with 'natural capital'.

INTERMEDIATE OUTPUT

A whole set of possible reforms in national income accounting can be derived from using the concept of 'intermediate output', which is already used in calculating GNP. Intermediate output consists of goods and services which are wanted not for their own sake but as means towards other goods and services ('final output'). Raw materials are generally wanted not for their own sake, but in order to make something. If both the materials and the final output were to be counted in GNP, the materials would be counted twice, once for themselves, and again when embodied in the final output. Existing national income accounting therefore excludes intermediate goods from national income totals.

However, the application of the concept of 'intermediate output' can be extended beyond its application in existing national income accounting. For example, Nordhaus and Tobin argued in 'Is Growth Obsolete?' that, 'No reasonable country (or household) buys "national defense" for its own sake. If there were no war or risk of war, there would be no need for defense expenditures and no one would be worse off without them. Conceptually then, defense expenditures are gross but not net output.'[4] They therefore propose subtracting this form of expenditure from GNP. 'From the point of view of economic welfare, an arms control or disarmament agreement which would free resources and raise consumption by 10 per cent would be just as significant as new industrial processes yielding the same gains.'[5] Excluding defence spending from GNP is a way of ensuring that such an improvement in circumstances would show up as an increase in GNP.

The same argument could be applied to expenditure on medicine and surgery, most of which is not desired for its own sake, but in response to undesirable changes in circumstances. An improvement in the circumstances (currently excluded from GNP) would be just as good as expenditure to compensate for undesirable circumstances (currently included in GNP).

Difficulties arise with this line of argument because there is a sense in which practically no goods or services are actually desired for their own sake, but are all desired as means to some other end. For example, transport is usually desired not because people like travelling, but as a means of getting from A to B, so that if B were to move nearer to A (e.g. a shop is opened nearer to where I live than the previous nearest shop) that would be just as good. Similarly, electricity for an electric fire is not desired for its own sake, but because of the heat it produces, so that a change in the weather would be just as good.

Once the argument for excluding intermediate output from national income is accepted in principle – and it is accepted in existing national accounting – then it is difficult to see where intermediate outputs stop and final outputs begin. Carrying the argument to its extreme, there are no goods which are final outputs, but only states of affairs: transport is a means towards access; electricity is a means towards warmth; defence expenditure can be a means towards security; medicine can be a means towards health, etc. These states of affairs are not, however, quantifiable in money terms, whereas the 'intermediate outputs' which can bring them about can be quantified in terms of money, and hence included in GNP. The concept of 'intermediate output' can therefore be used to argue for moving outside the framework of GNP to indicators which measure in non-money terms the states of affairs which traded goods and services are used to influence or buy. Within such a new framework, the whole of what is currently included in national income would be classified as 'intermediate output'.

ADJUSTED NATIONAL PRODUCT

The best proposal for adjusting the GNP or NNP figures to arrive at some form of adjusted national product would probably be one based on problems 1, 2, and 7 – unpaid domestic labour, non-money transactions outside the household, and environmental deterioration – and starting from net national product (as currently defined, i.e. GNP minus capital depreciation).

ANP would then be equal to: gross national product
minus capital depreciation
plus money value of unpaid domestic labour
plus money value of non-money transactions outside the household
minus environmental depreciation.

This has in its favour the fact that the problems of output not matched by income can be dealt with within the existing framework of national income accounting more easily than can problems about the relationship between output and welfare. Figures can be estimated for the money value of unpaid work (despite the problems referred to earlier in this chapter). It also seems very important to take into account environmental depreciation, since the failure to do so represents probably the most serious objection to national income accounting in its present form.

Whilst adjusted national product figures calculated on this basis would be a more sensible foundation for decision-making than the existing GNP figures are, there are a number of points to bear in mind about what they would *not* measure. First, this form of ANP would not provide an adequate measurement of welfare or of the economic component of welfare because it would not deal with all the other problems of national income accounting referred to in the previous chapter. For example, women's unpaid work would now be included, but women's paid work would still generally be undervalued in the (adjusted) national accounts in comparison to men's paid work because the wage rates and salary levels for comparable work are generally lower. Nor would this version of ANP deal with problems about the distribution of income (problem 3) or inefficiency in private provision and consumer decision-making (problems 12 and 13).

Second, it seems impossible to expand it into a form of ANP which deals with all the problems simultaneously. Some of the problems would be extremely difficult to quantify in money terms anyway (particularly the 'inefficiency' problems, 12 to 16). More fundamentally, when a series of different adjustments – such as sixteen different adjustments to deal with the sixteen different problems mentioned – are combined together, difficulties multiply and the outcome becomes less and less persuasive.

This is because each adjustment has implications for the others: they cannot each be made separately. Because the calculation of ANP is a money calculation, both in the case of the basic GNP and also the adjustments to it, a monetary value must be assigned to each adjustment. But in order to do this, there must be some 'real' monetary values to use as a basis. Some things need to have a price to provide the basis for imputed prices for other things. However, the greater the number of imputed or shadow prices being estimated relative to the number of 'real' prices, the more problematic and dubious the calculations become. Imputed prices come to be based on other imputed prices. For example, the value of depreciation to my washing machine (adjustment to deal with problem 6) comes to depend on what charges would be made at the local launderette if the distribution of income in the country were to be equalized (adjustment to deal with problem 3), *and* if the launderette had to put its prices up to compensate for the environmental depreciation caused by the detergents it uses (adjustment to deal with problem 7). The whole structure of such a reformed national income accounting would move further and further away from any observable real prices towards an increasingly abstract economists' theoretical construction, which would generate a wide variety of results for adjusted national product from different sets of definitions and assumptions.

Third, ANP isn't a way to measure sustainable income.[6] The national income level for a country which will prove to be sustainable in the long term is not something which can be known now, because it depends on so many unpredictable variables – climatic, technological, demographic, political, etc. – and therefore any figure for 'sustainable national income' is bound to be highly speculative. There is certainly no straightforward way in which current GNP or NNP can be adjusted to arrive at such a figure, by simply subtracting a value for environmental depreciation. It would be far more valid to *arrive at* the figure for environmental depreciation by first predicting sustainable national income and then comparing it with actual national income, with the difference between the two being environmental depreciation. The monetary value of environmental depreciation is not such a simple matter to calculate that it can be used as a short cut way of finding the sustainable level of national income.

Despite these reservations, it would nevertheless be better to use adjusted national product statistics to evaluate economic progress or welfare than to use the existing unadjusted gross national product figures. Measures to adjust GNP on the lines discussed in this chapter should therefore be encouraged, since they represent improvements. The most likely to happen in the near future appear to be adjustments to take account of some environmental costs.[6]

Looked at historically, however, the current attempt to calculate various forms of adjusted national product may well be looked back on primarily as a symptom of the decline of the dominance of GNP. In his classic discussion of paradigms in science, Thomas Kuhn made the point that elaborate arrays of adjustments and provisions for large numbers of exceptional cases are signs that a particular paradigm has lost its usefulness and is on the way out.[7]

In the next chapter, I shall try to locate national income accounting within the paradigm of mainstream economics, in order to show how a new paradigm for economics can generate a different set of indicators of welfare and progress.

5

GROWTH AND PROGRESS

The division between what is included within conventional economic indicators such as GNP and what is excluded from them is not random. There is a history to where the boundary line is drawn around 'economics', and around associated concepts such as 'production', 'work', and 'economic growth'. This chapter will seek to outline that history, and then argue for its use as a basis for identifying the areas where there is a particular need for alternative economic indicators.

In order to construct such a history, it is necessary to go back much further than the origins of national income accounting itself. The concept of economic growth is far older than the particular ways in which it is now measured. Current discussion of the validity and uses of GNP as a statistic should be placed within a larger context, as part of the long debate about 'Progress'.

The concept of 'Progress' can be traced back through many different routes to many different origins. Amongst these is the Jewish and Christian sense that human history has a particular meaning and purpose, a beginning and an end. This sense of history moving in a particular direction finds echoes and expressions in many of the major movements of thought in Western civilization, including Marxism, Darwinism, and growth-orientated economics, though in each case it is qualified and modified in a particular way.

The late eighteenth century and early nineteenth century saw the development of systems of thought which identified hope and Progress specifically with advances in science, technology, and industry. For example, Condorcet set out an optimistic analysis of human history divided into ten stages in his *Sketch for an Historical Picture of the Progress of the Human Mind* (published in 1795), in which the development of science played a crucial role, both in combating ignorance and superstition, and in bringing economic benefits. Saint-Simon produced a more complex but in the long term just as optimistic picture: 'the supreme law of progress of the human spirit carries along and dominates everything; men are but its instruments . . . it is no more in our power to withdraw ourselves from its influence or to control its action than it is to change at our pleasure the primitive impulse which makes our planet circle the sun'.[1] Again, science was seen as playing a major part in this process of historical advance, particularly through its application in technological innovation and in industry.

The most important of these theorists for the development of economics was Adam Smith. Smith's theory of historical progress has four stages, based on the development of the economy: hunting, pasturage, farming, and commercial society. In *The Wealth of Nations* (1776), Smith was centrally concerned with the analysis of economic advance ('the progress of opulence in different ages and nations'[2]), and with understanding its problems and its causes, including increases in the division of labour and the stock of capital accumulated.

The theories of progress presented by Condorcet, Saint-Simon, and Smith, were ones in which economic progress was seen as very closely linked to progress in science and technology, and the progress of the human mind and society in general. They were writing at a time of rapid economic and industrial change, trying to understand its significance and implications.

During the course of the nineteenth century, the construction of economics as a 'science' changed the debate about economic and human progress in important ways. All the major figures of nineteenth-century political economy – Malthus, Ricardo, Mill, and Marx, together with Adam Smith in the eighteenth century – discussed the economy in the context of society, the environment, and morality. Ricardo and Marx, particularly, were concerned with the ways in which returns to the different factors of production became reflected in the distribution of income between different classes of society, and the conflicts of interest which this created. Malthus was concerned with the limits which the natural world placed on the possibilities for growth in the economy and in population. All of them related economic issues directly to ethics. Eighteenth- and nineteenth-century political economy was, in general, a field of debate with a larger range of concerns than present-day economics.

The difference between nineteenth-century political economy and twentieth-century economics is essentially that the latter has been developed with the conscious intention of constructing a 'science', influenced by the models provided by the natural sciences of what a science *is*. The natural sciences had two features in particular which proved attractive to economists such as William Jevons and Alfred Marshall. First, the use of mathematics was seen as producing a more precise form of knowledge and a more logical structure of argument than could otherwise become available. Second, the emphasis was placed on explanations about what happens and what causes it, not on how morally to evaluate what happens.

It proved extraordinarily easy to establish economics as a quantitative 'science', much easier than parallel attempts to introduce mathematical precision into other social sciences. This was because money is inherently quantitative. Money can be added, subtracted, multiplied, and divided. If economics is about money, and being scientific is about being quantitative, then economics can be as scientific as physics. There was therefore a tendency for 'scientific' economics to be an economics centred on money. At the same time, the concept of 'utility' was used as a quantitative way of representing happiness, satisfaction, and welfare, connecting these with supply and demand, and hence with money.

In the process of developing a quantitative economics, some parts of the understanding of what the economy was which had been central to eighteenth- and nineteenth-century political economy came to be marginalized or even excluded from the discipline. Moral evaluation came to be regarded as not 'scientific', and was not generally thought to be amenable to quantitative methods (except for the stricter varieties of utilitarianism). The price of labour and its products became a central part of economics, but the fact that labour is contributed and carried out by human beings tended not to be a focus of attention, the study of the organization and experience of the process of labour being regarded as a matter for sociologists and psychologists rather than economists. Supply and demand for raw materials is certainly part of economics, but the question of whether there are physical and biological limits to the availability of raw materials and the absorption of waste products tends to be seen as a matter for geologists and biologists, not part of the subject-matter of economics.

At the same time, however, twentieth-century economic debate has tended to continue with basically the same underlying conceptions of economic progress as those developed in the late eighteenth century. The same general beliefs remain about science, technology, and the identification of economic progress with human and social progress in general. Something, however, has been added: for economics as a developing quantitative science, gross national product statistics appeared to offer a much more precise way of talking about economic progress.

The result of the changes which have taken place in economics is that we now have a high degree of precision in the measurement of one particular form of progress – growth in GNP – but a failure to appreciate sufficiently the need to situate that form of progress within its larger human and natural context. The smaller, more focused, more precise, part of discourse about economic progress – national income accounting – has become a very respectable part of economics. The issues about how this form of progress is related to Progress in a much larger sense – moral, human, social – are not much debated in the economic journals.

This would not be such a serious problem if there was a close connection between GNP growth rates and the other varieties of progress. Growth in GNP could then function as the representative of a much larger category. In fact, however, high growth rates are often the result of high human and environmental costs of production. In these situations, economic 'progress' is taking place at the expense of progress in other areas.

The three main areas which have been marginalized or excluded in the transition from nineteenth-century political economy to twentieth-century economic 'science' are:

1 'human economics' – the economy seen as grounded in the lives of human beings, in our roles as producers, consumers, members of families, citizens, etc.;
2 'natural economics' – the economy seen as grounded in natural resources and the biological and physical processes of the natural world; and

3 the economy seen as something for which moral evaluation is relevant.

These three areas are exactly those which have raised problems about the desirability and sustainability of continued economic growth, and the relationship between economic growth and 'progress' in its wider senses. There is therefore a correspondence between the topics which were part of political economy and became excluded or marginalized, and the topics which are now the concerns of those who raise problems about growth. In order to consider and discuss those problems adequately within economics, the scope and emphases of economics needs to be changed. Such a reorientation of economics would effectively amount to the revival and renewal of political economy.

THREE WAYS OF DESCRIBING ECONOMIC PROCESSES

Within an enlarged economics – or a renewed political economy – there would be three parallel ways of describing economic processes:

1 the economy considered from a monetary or *financial* point of view (which is the one emphasized by present-day economics);
2 the economy considered as consisting of *human* beings organized together in particular ways; and
3 the economy considered as a set of arrangements for mediating the relationship between human beings and the *natural* world.

What happens in the economy can validly be given descriptions of all three types. For example, the importing of food into a country can be viewed in terms of a flow of money to pay for it and the representation of that flow in the balance of payments statistics, as a social relationship of (perhaps unequal) interdependence between trading partners, and as a means by which people in one location can make use of resources located somewhere else.

Corresponding to these three perspectives on the economy – financial, human, and natural – there are three different

46

types of indicators. Existing economic indicators such as those associated with national income and balance of payments accounting, look at the economy from a financial perspective, measuring monetary flows through a national economy or between different national economies.

But the economy can also be measured from the perspectives of 'human economics' and 'natural economics' if appropriate indicators are selected for these purposes. What these indicators might be is the main concern of the next three chapters of this book. Chapter 6, the next chapter, discusses the general question: 'what makes a good indicator?' Chapter 7 looks at indicators of society and the human economy. Chapter 8 discusses indicators of the environment and the natural economy.

6

THE GOOD INDICATOR

The 'human' and 'natural' perspectives on economics imply the use of social and environmental indicators to measure economic performance, alongside money indicators such as balance of payments and GNP statistics. Economies do not exist in isolation or purely for their own sake. They have effects on society and the environment, and society and the environment provide the inputs which economies use (labour, natural resources, etc.).

In order to move from this stage in the argument to a discussion of specific indicators, it is necessary to consider now the criteria which should be used to select the best indicators. I will start by looking at some possible criteria which I think should *not* be used, even though they may appear at first sight to be amongst the most obvious ones.

First, an indicator should not have to carry with it an automatic evaluation. I mean by this that it doesn't have to be always 'good' if it goes up, always 'bad' if it comes down, or always 'good' if it comes down and 'bad' if it goes up. For example, the proportion of the population aged 65 and over is (or perhaps is not) a significant indicator, regardless of whether anyone thinks it is a good thing for the proportion to be high, or a good thing if it is low. It simply tells us something which we may regard as important. Indicators should reflect reality, not only present those aspects of reality which can be evaluated easily.

Second, an indicator should not have to have a policy instrument which corresponds to it. The best policy to respond to the information given by an indicator may be difficult to formulate, and controversial, and even the best policy may not make a lot of difference. We should not assume that it is necessary to match the self-assurance of those economists who believe that every economic problem has a corresponding policy to correct it. Again, indicators should reflect reality, not simply present those aspects which it is easy to know how to respond to.

Third, an indicator doesn't have to be new. If careful consideration of possible indicators leads to the choice of some which are very familiar (though not necessarily to economists), such as the infant mortality rate, then there is nothing wrong with that. Readers of this book who are expecting me to come up with an entirely new set of indicators are going to be disappointed, because in many cases I believe there are good grounds for choosing indicators which already exist. The key difference of opinion between this book and many others is that measuring changes in social and environmental indicators (and not just financial indicators) is put forward here as a valid means of evaluating economies and economic policies.

Fourth, proposals for sets of indicators based on particular theories of economic, social, and human development and 'true' (as opposed to supposedly 'false') human needs are open to a lot of objections, particularly when they are based on the assumption that there is only one path of development which is valid. Examples of this outlook include development theories which assume that 'economic development' must mean becoming more and more like the most urbanized and polluted areas of the USA, and that 'human development' means that no aesthetic or 'self-actualization' needs can be met until physiological needs have been fully satisfied first. Such views are too restrictive to correspond to the variety of routes that economic and human development actually take.

I would like to propose instead of these four criteria which I do not believe should be used, *seven criteria for a good indicator:*

1 The indicator itself, or the information it is calculated from, should be already available, or else able to be made available easily and cheaply. This is particularly important for Third World countries, where the resources to collect and process statistical information are strictly limited. Proposed indicators which are difficult and/or expensive to collect the information for are much less likely to be put into practice than indicators for which the information can be easily and cheaply collected. Other factors may outweigh this consideration, but it is clearly an important one.

2 The indicator should be relatively easy to understand. The more widespread such understanding is, the less likely it will be that people will be misled by economists, politicians, and others. Indicators which are the outcome of many complex mathematical adjustments are liable to be much more difficult to understand, and seem much less 'real' and significant than those which appear as the straightforward reporting of a fact. This consideration is one reason for being sceptical about proposals for adjusted national products and overall indices of development, and preferring instead to highlight figures for *'real indicators'* of specific things such as the rate of population increase or the rate of forest destruction per year.

3 The indicator, to work at all, must be about something measurable. 'The loss of community' cannot be an indicator. We can try to find ways of measuring it by looking at the suicide rate, the rate at which people move house, the extent to which people living in the same area influence each other's voting behaviour, etc., because all these are quantitatively measurable things. But 'the loss of community' (like many other things) is not itself directly measurable and therefore, however important it may be, it is not an indicator.

4 Perhaps most obvious of all, an indicator should measure something believed to be important or significant in its own right, or should reflect or represent something important beyond what the indicator is itself a measurement of (for example, life expectancy figures might be used to indicate the general state of health of the population). This is really what makes something an *indicator*, rather than just a statistic. Often this implies that an indicator will be chosen because it measures or represents something widely felt to be a problem. If water pollution isn't a problem, it won't seem important enough to make a measurement of it a major indicator. One way to build up a set of indicators is to decide which are the most important problems to keep track of (this approach is basically the one adopted in chapter 8 in looking at environmental indicators).

5 There should preferably only be a short time-lag between the state of affairs referred to and the indicator becoming

available (though this is often not so much a matter of which indicator is chosen, but more to do with the efficiency or staffing levels amongst the statisticians doing the work). It would be useful if some indicators could be found which would act as 'early warning signals' about states of affairs likely or possible in the future.

6 It is useful if the indicator is based on information which can be used to compare different geographical areas, social groups, etc., so that a picture of distribution – and not just totals and averages – can be built up.

7 International comparability is desirable, though difficult to achieve because of differences in environmental circumstances and social institutions. The main emphasis in this book is on trying to find a single set of indicators for use internationally, but from this set different indicators will be more significant in some countries than in others, and there will be many cases where there is a need to highlight additional indicators not relevant for worldwide comparisons. It does not, however, invalidate an indicator for purposes of international comparison if some countries score close to 0 per cent or 100 per cent of what is possible, whilst others consistently score much more or much less (for example, percentage of the population with access to safe drinking water, or literacy rates). This simply brings out the range of difference which exists in the world, particularly between richer countries and poorer countries. It would be wrong to exclude any indicators on the grounds that the contrasts they show are too stark, and to say that completely separate sets of indicators should be regarded as appropriate for rich and poor nations. This would militate against making comparisons which are important ones to make.

In addition to these criteria, the list of recommended indicators argued for in this book is also influenced by the desire to be selective, so as to focus attention on a fairly small set of *priority* indicators. The aim is to highlight what is most significant, rather than to include everything.

ARE SUBJECTIVE INDICATORS GOOD INDICATORS?

One possible basis for a set of indicators is to ground it in people's subjective feelings or perceptions. The public's rating of the significance of various factors can be used as a means of arriving at a corresponding set of indicators.

The relevant information here is provided by research into public opinion, where a representative sample of the population is asked to rate factors such as housing, income, and working conditions, according to the importance of each for their own happiness or well-being, and then to say whether they think there have been improvements recently (e.g. over the past year) in each factor. Indicators based on information of this sort can be described as 'subjective indicators'.

The UK Government publication *Social Trends*, though mainly concerned with 'objective' statistics, such as average incomes, numbers of hospital beds, etc., also published in the 1970s some material on subjective indicators. In the 1973 edition, Mark Abrams discussed attempts in both the UK and USA to measure 'the degree of satisfaction or dissatisfaction felt by people with various aspects of their lives'.[1] In the 1976 *Social Trends*, John Hall reviewed some further work on the subject, centred around attempts to measure people's perceptions of their quality of life.[2]

The 1973 article reported on a survey carried out in November 1971 on a sample of people in the seven largest conurbations in Britain, in which they were asked to rate their level of satisfaction in a series of 'domains' (family life, health, standard of living, etc.) and to rate the importance of each domain for their overall level of satisfaction. This showed that people generally rated their marriage as both more satisfactory, and more important to their overall satisfaction, than any other area of life. 'Standard of living' was seen as fourth (out of eleven areas) in importance, and eighth in satisfactoriness.[3]

Information of this sort can be used to put specifically economic factors in the wider context of all the different influences on people's sense of their own well-being. It would be possible, for example, to measure whether or not improvements in reported satisfaction with standard of living and job were outweighed in importance to people by deteriorations in other areas of life. One might also use this information to argue that political debate should focus more on issues concerning the quality of marriage and family life (first and second in importance, respectively, in the 1971 survey) and less on areas rated by the public as less important.

John Hall, in the 1976 *Social Trends*, explores the idea of looking for correlations between subjective and objective indicators to see what effects various changes in circumstances have on changes in reported satisfaction. For example, improvements in housing conditions seem likely to have an effect on reported satisfaction with housing. Hall suggests that 'subjective indicators may be used to weight objective indicators' – which would make it possible to say, for example, whether fewer households having to share a kitchen would be a more significant improvement than fewer households sharing a bathroom.[4]

A similar approach, combining subjective and objective indicators, was adopted in a 1988 study of *Quality of Life in British Cities* by researchers at Glasgow University. They used fifty-two indicators of quality of life, grouped into 'dimensions' (e.g. shopping facilities, levels of pollution), which were weighted according to 'the perceived importance of each of these dimensions as reported in the national opinion survey of a representative sample of 1200 respondents'. 'The outcome is therefore a ranking of British cities in terms of the availability of those characteristics determined by the average British citizen to be the most important dimensions of quality of life.'[5] Out of thirty-eight urban areas with a population over 250,000, the survey rated Edinburgh first and London thirty-fourth.

There are, however, a number of problems with using people's reports of their own happiness or satisfaction as the basis for developing indicators. People may want to claim to others, including the survey interviewer, a greater degree of satisfaction with various aspects of life than is actually the case. There may be cultural differences between different societies in how readily people are willing to report unhappiness or dissatisfaction (a 1981 survey found 38 per cent of British people willing to describe themselves as 'very happy', but only 10 per cent of West Germans were willing to describe themselves in the same way).[6] There are likely to be enormous international differences in the standards felt to be a 'realistic' basis for 'satisfaction' or 'dissatisfaction'. And 'satisfaction' may represent adaptation to adverse circumstances, and the loss of any sense that they could be different, rather than any improvement in circumstances.

Another problem with this approach is that people may not perceive the importance to themselves of factors which require quite a lot of information to understand. For example, a survey might show that the majority of people are not much concerned about the balance of payments – but it does not necessarily follow that 'subjective economic indicators' should therefore advise the Government to ignore it and concentrate only on features of the economy which people report as directly concerning them, such as rates of inflation and levels of wages. Subjective indicators can easily become a way of measuring the amount of publicity there has been about something, or how informed people are on different subjects. For example, the recent increase in concern about the ozone layer, which would show up in subjective indicators as having a greater importance attached to it, reflects more an increase in publicity and in availability of information on the subject, rather than a change in the state of the ozone layer itself.

There are circumstances in which subjective indicators are useful, but – largely because this book is concerned with making international comparisons – the approach adopted here is to concentrate on 'objective' indicators. The next two chapters discuss specifically which indicators should be selected as priorities.

7

SOCIAL INDICATORS

Chapter 5 argued for an expanded conception of economics, which would amount to a 'renewal of political economy'. Corresponding to this, an expanded framework of economic indicators was proposed, consisting of three areas: financial indicators (such as GNP and the balance of payments), 'natural indicators' of the environment and natural resources, and 'human indicators' of the human aspects of the economy. Almost every element in the economy has these three aspects – money changes hands, there is some interaction with the environment, and human beings are affected in some way – and all three can be reflected in quantitative indicators.

This chapter is concerned with human, or social, indicators. It looks in particular at: education and literacy, work and unemployment, consumption, the distribution of income and wealth, and health. Indicators of each of these can provide yardsticks for measuring the 'success', 'progress', and 'efficiency' of the economy, if these terms are defined in more than a purely financial way. Statistics for my proposed 'priority indicators' for fourteen countries, where available, are set out in chapter 9.

INDICATORS OF EDUCATION AND LITERACY

Education and literacy are obviously important. They are virtually essential for democratic participation in society, especially if it is to be beyond the scale of a small local community. In many societies, they are necessary both to cope with everyday tasks like filling in forms and to get access to the arts and sciences which those societies have created or learned

55

from. Education and literacy influence the 'quality' of labour because they are important determinants of the level of skill in an economy. Education and literacy amongst women and girls are key influences on the understanding of information about contraception, and therefore on both the birth rate and the level of female participation in the paid labour force; they also influence the distribution of income between women and men and the status of women in society.

In choosing a set of priority indicators, one possibility for inclusion is school enrolment ratios. These are defined as 'the number of children enrolled in primary or secondary school (regardless of age) as a percentage of the total number of children in the relevant age group for that level'.[1] But this assumes an orderly and simple relationship between age group and level of education. In many countries, the figures for primary school enrolment in fact reach more than 100 per cent, because many children of 'secondary school age' attend primary schools.

In order to get round this problem, *net* enrolment ratios can be calculated, showing 'the total number of children enrolled in a schooling level who belong in the relevant age group, expressed as a percentage of the total number of children in that age group'.[2] In the case of the secondary school net enrolment ratio, there is a further problem, however, which is that the figures to a large extent reflect whether or not a country has a non-compulsory stage of secondary education (like the English sixth-forms) – something which is not necessarily an indication of a low general level of education. The indicator recommended here is therefore the *net enrolment ratio for primary schools*.

'Adult literacy' refers to the percentage of people over the age of 15 who can read and write. Statistics on this – and on school enrolment – are collected and published by the United Nations Educational, Scientific and Cultural Organization (UNESCO). 'UNESCO recommends defining a person as illiterate when she or he cannot with understanding both read and write a short simple statement on her or his everyday life'.[3] Although the interpretation of this definition can vary in different countries and at different times, figures for the number of *illiterate adults as a percentage of the adult population* nevertheless give an overall indication of something extremely important. In some respects, literacy figures are more significant than school enrolment ratios, because they represent the outcome of schooling (and of less formalized ways of learning), rather than simply the 'input' of the quantity of schooling itself, which might or might not have been effective as a form of education.

Because of wide differences in figures for females and males in many countries, as regards both education and literacy, and because of the significance of these differences, ratios for females and males are given separately.

INDICATORS OF WORK AND UNEMPLOYMENT

Work is important both to individuals' lives and to whole economies. National income accounting in its current form provides data about work on the basis of income received from it. This has two implications: only work which is paid for is counted, with unpaid work excluded; and the work which is counted is quantified in money terms rather than in some other way, such as average number of hours worked per week.

Problems of national income accounting were discussed in chapter 3. It follows from the arguments set out there that there is a need for indicators of work quantified in some terms other than money, and time spent is the obvious alternative to choose. Moving away from the focus on money which is inherent in national income accounting also removes any justification for excluding unpaid work from indicators of work. The arguments for including unpaid work, such as most housework, childcare, and much subsistence agricultural work, are clear: it takes time and effort just as paid work does, it is generally just as demanding (and often more so), it consists of exactly the same activities as much of paid work consists of, and it can be measured in the same units (e.g. average hours per week). Including unpaid work in indicators of quantity of work also has the major advantage of giving a much more realistic account of the distribution of work as between women and men than is presented by figures for paid work only.

Economic data which excludes unpaid work can only be regarded as partial and incomplete, in view of both the time spent on unpaid work and its importance for society. A recent International Labour Organization (ILO) study, *Assessing Women's Economic Contributions to Development*, concludes that 'available estimates for developing countries suggest that domestic activities account for approximately 40 to 45 per cent of total labour time of all household members'.[3] Similar figures are implied by BBC surveys for time use in the UK.[4]

Surveys of time use which have been carried out generally produce different figures for the same person at different times, because of seasonal variations, such as school holidays and variations in agricultural work. Such surveys often only provide for someone carrying out one ('primary') activity at a time, when in practice two or more activities are often carried out simultaneously. Since childcare is often a 'secondary' activity combined with other things, it tends to be under-recorded in such studies.

Yet this and other problems (some of which were referred to in chapter 4) are far less significant than the problems involved in excluding unpaid work from economic accounting. The most important difficulty, however, with the use of indicators of total work (both paid and unpaid) is that the data is simply not currently available. *Assessing Women's Economic Contributions to Development* found that: 'time-use surveys are difficult and expensive to conduct. Almost always restricted to specific locales with relatively small samples, they are rarely generalisable to national populations.'[5] Two ILO studies specifically on unpaid household work provide general reviews of such surveys, but they do not provide data systematically for whole countries.[6]

Even figures for paid work are not available on a comprehensive basis. Since national income accounts are usually based largely on tax returns, much paid work goes unrecorded. Some countries include in their national accounts estimates for the 'informal' money economy, much of it criminal or semi-criminal.

Within the formal paid sector, data is often not available for agricultural work. The main international publication for labour statistics, the ILO *Year Book of Labour Statistics*, gives figures for average hours worked per week per wage earner in (paid) non-agricultural activities (figures for the Group of Seven countries for 1987, excluding Italy which instead produces figures for average hours per day, ranged from 43.1 hours per week for the UK to 32.0 for Canada). But even then it does not provide figures for most Third World countries.

Figures are, however, generally available for the percentage *rate of unemployment*, seen as involuntary exclusion from income-earning. Here there are problems of international comparability, because different governments use different methods and definitions for arriving at the unemployment figures they publish. Some standardization has, however, been achieved by using the definitions adopted by the International Labour Organization, and also used by the Organization for Economic Co-operation and Development. These include only those people who have sought and not done any paid work within the past four weeks.

INDICATORS OF CONSUMPTION

National income accounting makes it possible to measure consumption in terms of GNP per capita, i.e. GNP divided by population. Another way to measure consumption levels is in terms of goods and services which are in some way essential and 'basic', or are representative of a large and significant category. Three such indicators of consumption are proposed here, covering food, water supply, and telephones.

Consumption of food can be measured in terms of average per capita supplies per day, in calories. These figures become more significant when combined with figures for the minimum number of calories required per capita per day, which are different for different countries. The indicator of food consumption which I propose to highlight here is the ratio between these two figures: *calorie supply as a percentage of minimum requirements*.

The minimum daily calorie requirements per capita are calculated by the World Health Organization (WHO), 'which takes into account body size, age and sex distribution, physical activity, level of the population, climate, and other factors'.[7] These range from 2,710 for Finland to 2,160 for Burma.[8] The UN Food and Agriculture Organization (FAO) compiles figures for food available for human consumption in terms of energy equivalent (calories), per capita per day (including imports but excluding exports). Some of this, however, may be 'lost in home storage, preparation and cooking in addition to what is fed to pets and domestic animals or is discarded'.[7] Particularly high calorie consumption figures are, of course, no more desirable than low figures, because of the danger of heart disease and other health problems, but a 100 per cent rating represents

59

the achievement of just the minimum requirement and so the problems of high calorie consumption do not become serious until some way above this figure.

Figures for *percentage of the population with access to safe drinking water* are compiled by the World Health Organization on the basis of information provided by national governments. 'Access' in urban areas means that there is a source within 200 metres of where someone lives, and in rural areas that 'members of the household do not have to spend a disproportionate part of the day fetching water'. 'Safe' includes surface water which has been treated, and water from springs, sanitary wells, and protected boreholes which is untreated but uncontaminated.[9]

Telephones in use per thousand people is a good indicator of the degree of economic 'development' in a society, at a more advanced level than is signified by the availability of clean water and an adequate calorie supply. Accurate figures are available for this indicator for almost all countries.

Another possible indicator could be some measurement of energy consumption, which can be seen as representative of a large and important category of forms of consumption. The problem about this, however, is the wide disparity in the efficiency with which energy is used in different countries, and therefore the wide range of different levels of overall consumption which the same energy consumption per capita figure represents. I am therefore not proposing this as an indicator of consumption levels. Another energy indicator – 'energy intensity' – is discussed in chapter 8.

INDICATORS OF DISTRIBUTION OF INCOME AND WEALTH

Indicators for the distribution of income are important but problematic. The figures compiled by the World Bank refer to: 'Income (both in cash and kind) accruing to percentile groups of households ranked by total household income.'[9] Figures for different countries vary partly according to how comprehensively 'income in kind' is defined. The extent of inequality between household incomes may give a misleading impression of inequality in individual incomes because households may have large incomes as a result of being large households rather than because the average individual income of their members is high. Furthermore, the distribution of income by household gives no information about the distribution of income amongst individual members within households. Despite these serious problems, it again seems to be the case that what these indicators refer to is so important that it is right to highlight them, particularly in the absence of more reliable internationally comparable information.

The World Bank publish figures for the percentage of all household income received by the 10 per cent of households with the highest incomes, the highest 20 per cent, the lowest 40 per cent, and the lowest 20 per cent.[10] Rather than highlight all four of these indicators, an overall measure of the extent to which income distribution differs from an equal distribution is provided by the ratio of upper and lower quintiles, i.e. the *income received by the top 20 per cent divided by the income received by the bottom 20 per cent*.

To obtain a more complete picture, this indicator needs to be considered in conjunction with figures for the distribution of wealth (partly because wealth can function as a substitute for income). The most easily comparable indicator would be marketable wealth owned by the top 20 per cent of households divided by the marketable wealth owned by the bottom 20 per cent. This and similar information about wealth distribution is, however, not available in the vast majority of cases, and therefore unfortunately cannot be included in the list of recommended indicators. It is nevertheless important to argue for the collection and publication of this data so that it can be added to the list later. It is difficult to see how sensible decisions can be made about economic policies and development strategies without the information necessary to assess the impact on the distribution of wealth.

HEALTH INDICATORS

Figures are available for a large number of different health and mortality indicators. One of these is the crude death rate, which is defined as the number of deaths occurring in a year per thousand people in the population in the middle of that year. For example, in a country of 50 million people, a crude death rate of 12 signifies a total number of deaths of 50,000 multiplied by 12, i.e. 600,000.

It might be thought possible to use the death rate as an indicator of the overall standard of health. However, there is an important way in which crude death rate statistics are highly misleading. Figures for death rates of people in specific age groups show the obvious fact that, in general, older people are more likely to die in any given year than younger people (often with the exception of babies, who also have a high death rate in many parts of the world). Therefore, the higher the average age in a particular country, the higher its death rate is likely to be. A fall in the death rate may reflect a fall in the average age, rather than improvements in public health, consumption patterns, medicine, etc. In fact, the better people's health, the higher the average age is likely to be because people will tend to live for longer, and so the higher the crude death rate. This makes it a very poor indicator, because increases may reflect both improvements and deteriorations in health.

Another approach is to consider life expectancy at birth. The major difficulty with this is that whether or not someone dies in a particular year depends on events and circumstances over a long period of time, not simply in that particular year. Whether someone who is 70 years old will survive to 71 or not depends on a large set of factors over the whole of their lives. There is therefore a built-in time-lag, of the order of 35 years, between cause and effect. Life expectancy and death rates for specific age groups for this year mainly reflect circumstances decades ago. Similarly changes in behaviour and policy now may not show up in the figures on a large scale for at least a decade.

The only way round this problem – since it is not possible to estimate accurately the effects of current changes on future life expectancy and future age-specific death rate figures – is to take the age-specific death rate for the age group with the shortest gap of time between death and birth, which must be the youngest age group.

This information is provided by the *infant mortality rate* (IMR), which is defined as the number of deaths under one year of age during a year, per thousand live births during that year. This information is collected by the United Nations Population Division and the UN Statistical Office. The IMR suffers from neither the problem of variations in age distribution, nor the problem of long time-lags. Changes in the IMR quickly

62

reflect changes in production, consumption, and environmental circumstances.

In fact, the IMR is particularly sensitive to such changes. According to the World Health Organization: 'The IMR not only reflects the magnitude of those health problems which are directly responsible for the deaths of infants, such as diarrhoeal and respiratory infections and malnutrition, along with other specific infectious diseases and perinatal conditions, but it also reflects the level of health of mothers, the level of antenatal and postnatal care of mother and infant, family planning policy, the environmental health situation and, in general, the socioeconomic development of a society.'[11] Another way of putting essentially the same point is that 'it reflects the experience of particularly sensitive and vulnerable subjects who might be expected to be the first to be affected by detrimental changes (I mean of course the mother, the fetus and the infant)'.[12]

Going further, a Worldwatch Institute publication on infant mortality argued that: 'The most decisive gains to be made in moving a country from high to moderate infant mortality rates involve improvements in the direct causes of infant death – better sanitation, water supply, nutrition, access to fertility control and medical care, and education. Clearly, policies that accomplish these goals will confer great benefits on society as a whole. A reduction in the infant mortality rate therefore sends a double signal: not only has a major humanitarian goal been realized, but the general process of national development is moving in a healthy direction.'[13]

The same arguments apply to the *under-five mortality rate* (U5MR), which is the number of deaths under five years of age during a year per thousand live births. This is also collected by the UN Population Division and UN Statistical Office, and has been chosen by the United Nations Children's Fund (UNICEF) as 'its single most important indicator of the state of a nation's children'. UNICEF also propose using the average annual rate of reduction in U5MR as one way of measuring social progress.

They point out that 'U5MR is less susceptible than, say, per capita GNP to the fallacy of the average. This is because the natural scale does not allow the children of the rich to be one thousand times as likely to survive, even if the man-made scale does permit them to have one thousand times as much income. In other words, it is much more difficult for a wealthy minority to affect a nation's U5MR, and it therefore presents a more accurate, if far from perfect, picture of the health status of the majority of children (and of society as a whole)'.[14]

CONCLUSIONS

The set of priority human or social indicators which has emerged from the 'seven criteria for a good indicator' set out in the previous chapter, and the discussion of possible indicators in this chapter, is as follows:

1 Net primary school enrolment ratio for girls.
2 Net primary school enrolment ratio for boys.
3 Female illiteracy rate.
4 Male illiteracy rate.
5 The rate of unemployment.
6 Average calorie supply as a percentage of requirements.
7 Percentage of the population with access to safe drinking water.
8 Telephones per thousand people.
9 Household income received by the top 20 per cent of households divided by that received by the bottom 20 per cent.
10 Infant mortality rate.
11 Under-five mortality rate.

One way of conceiving of the relationship between these indicators is to see the first five as (amongst other things) indicators of the input of labour into the economy, or in other words, indicators of the human economy from the perspective of people as *producers*; indicators 6, 7, 8, and 9 as indicators of the human economy from the perspective of people in their role as *consumers*; and indicators 10 and 11 as indicators of the human economy from the perspective of the *effects* which production and consumption have on people.

In addition, data should be collected to make it possible to add two further indicators: average hours worked per week (including both paid and unpaid work), and marketable wealth owned by the top 20 per cent of households divided by that owned by the bottom 20 per cent.

8

ENVIRONMENTAL INDICATORS

ENVIRONMENTAL ACCOUNTING

Some governments have established, or begun to establish, systems of environmental accounting. These systems follow the same general pattern as company financial accounts. For each resource, there is an opening figure for the total stock of that resource at the start of the accounting period, then figures for the amount of the resource that have been used up, and any additions to stock, and finally a figure for the total stock of the resource at the end of the period. For example:

Area of forest, January 1st	1,000 sq. km
Minus: Forest cut down during the year	70 sq. km
Plus: New forest planted	20 sq. km
Equals: Area of forest, December 31st	950 sq. km

Accounts can be compiled with the opening figure as the state of a resource (e.g. water quality), an 'income' figure for the addition of pollutants, an 'expenditure' figure for the effect of purification processes, and a final figure for the state of the resource at the end of the period.

It is also possible to link environmental accounts to national income accounts by including prices and price changes, thereby converting physical measurements (e.g. 1,000 square kilometres) into money terms. Results from this could then be used to calculate an adjusted national product figure (discussed in chapter 4).

The country with the most developed system of environmental accounting is Norway, where the accounts are divided into 'mineral resources', 'biological resources', 'inflowing resources' (solar radiation, wind, ocean currents, etc.), and 'environmental resources' (air, water, soil, space). Environmental accounting is also used in France and Canada.[1]

These systems of accounting provide frameworks for the collection of data on natural and environmental resources which make it possible to build up a comprehensive picture. Unlike national income accounting (but like company accounting), they are concerned as much with total stocks of 'assets' as with flows in and out during a particular period of time.

Whilst environmental accounting adds to, and organizes, the available data in useful ways, it is of limited value for the purposes of this book, which is concerned not with the development of a comprehensive framework but with the selection of a small set of priority indicators. The aim is to produce 'headline figures' which can rival the GNP growth rate, rather than a rival to the whole system of national income accounting. Such 'headline figures' cannot be derived from environmental accounting as a whole, because the only meaningful way to add all environmental and natural resources together is in money terms, which takes us back to the national income accounting framework and therefore to its problems. The alternative to this is to select from amongst the mass of environmental data (whether it is organized into a full-scale environmental accounting system or not) a small set of figures which represent the most important current facts about the environment. This is the alternative I have adopted in this chapter.

TROPICAL DEFORESTATION

One of the most serious problems currently facing the world is the destruction of tropical forests. The effects of this include major contributions to the extinction of species and to the greenhouse effect (see the separate sections on these issues), flooding, droughts, damage to the lives of native peoples, and reduction of the potential to use forest resources to produce economically useful products in the future.

The indicator I propose to use is *rate of tropical deforestation in square kilometres per year*. The major problem about this – and any other indicators of deforestation – is the lack of available reliable data. The Worldwatch Institute's *State of the World 1988* says: 'Despite growing recognition of the importance of forests to the economic and ecological health of nations, surprisingly little is known with certainty about the state of forest resources today. Many countries have not fully inventoried their forests, and the data that do exist vary widely in quality.'[2] There is no deforestation indicator which could be selected that would get round this problem. There is simply an urgent need for more reliable, comprehensive, and up-to-date data.

Estimates from different surveys differ partly because some rely on government sources, others on non-government organizations; and some have an economic focus, being concerned primarily with timber production, whilst others have an ecological focus, concerned with the forest as an ecosystem in which trees are the most important, but not the only, element. There is also a matter of degree: at what point is damage to forest sufficiently great for it to count as 'deforestation'? The most comprehensive survey of deforestation ever undertaken is currently being carried out by the UN Food and Agriculture Organization, and will be published in 1992 or 1993.

The figures given in chapter 9 are estimates by Dr Norman Myers, in a report published in 1989, *Deforestation Rates in Tropical Forests and Their Climatic Implications*. The focus of the report is ecological, and there is 'an emphasis on non-governmental sources of documentation' which, it argues, are generally more reliable (as well as being more pessimistic).[3]

Forests outside tropical areas are generally less subject to deforestation, and more reforestation takes place. The forests themselves are very different from tropical forests, and they suffer mainly from a different problem: damage to trees caused by acid rain, rather than wholesale clearing of forest area. Deforestation in terms of area lost is a far less appropriate indicator than in the case of tropical forests.

EXTINCTION OF SPECIES

The world is currently living through a period of mass extinction of species, reducing the ability of the natural world to carry out the various forms of mainly unseen labour it is easy to take for granted but which are the foundation of all human life and all economies: the absorption of waste, the recycling of nutrients, the creation of soil, the cleaning of the air, and the storage and circulation of water. Many individual species have existing or potential future medical, nutritional, and industrial applications, and so extinction has a direct economic cost. And species have an intrinsic value, beyond their value for human beings.

The most obvious indicator to use to measure the scale of this extinction is the number of species lost per year. It might also be possible to convert this into a figure for the annual percentage rate of species lost.

There are problems about using species as an indicator. First, there is not complete agreement amongst scientists about the classifications involved: what one biologist might count as a species, another might consider to be merely a sub-species. Second, it may not be the number of species which is primarily important for the maintenance of the diversity of life: it may be far more significant that whole genera or families exist or become extinct than that individual species do. Third, counts simply of the number of species implicitly value all equally, whereas some species might be considered more important than others, for economic, ecological, evolutionary, or other reasons. Fourth, at what point can a species be counted as extinct? Just because it hasn't been seen by humans for a year or two, it cannot necessarily be assumed to have disappeared. Whatever time-period we require before we are prepared to say that something is extinct (10 years? 50 years? 100 years?) will be crucial in determining what the extinction rate is calculated to be at any particular time.

More serious than these problems, however, is the fact that the information is simply not available. There are no reliable figures even for the total existing number of species. Estimates currently vary from 4 million to over 30 million.[4] It is estimated that at least 10 to 15 per cent of all plants remain undiscovered, perhaps 10 per cent of fish species, and possibly 97 per cent of insects.[5] It is therefore impossible to give any total figures for particular countries in particular years for the rate at which species are disappearing.

Rough global estimates can nevertheless be given, based mainly on changes in the areas of habitats, such as patches of tropical rainforest, coral reefs, etc. Professor E. O. Wilson says that he has 'conservatively estimated that on a worldwide basis the ultimate loss attributable to rain-forest clearing alone . . . is from .2 to .3 per cent of all species in the forests per year.'[6] The Brundtland Report refers to another ecological zone in which there is a high extinction rate: 'Coral reefs, with an estimated half-million species . . . are being depleted at rates that may leave little but degraded remnants by early next century.'[7] The 1980 US study, *The Global 2000 Report to the President* estimated overall that 'of the 3–10 million species now present on the earth, at least 500,000–600,000 will be extinguished during the next two decades'.[8] In percentage terms, this works out at somewhere between a quarter of a per cent and one per cent, per year (or one species every twenty minutes).

As a result of the large gaps in the data, I do not propose to include the extinction rate as one of this book's recommended indicators. It would nevertheless be desirable to include it if and when fuller data becomes available. Since estimates for overall extinction rates are derived mainly from estimates for what is happening to habitats – above all, to tropical forests, which are rich in species – probably in the mean time the best proxy to use for extinction rate is the rate of tropical deforestation.

THE GREENHOUSE EFFECT

The build-up of greenhouse gases (carbon dioxide, methane, tropospheric ozone, CFCs, etc.) in the atmosphere is warming the earth by increasingly preventing heat from escaping. With no greenhouse gases, it has been estimated that the earth would be 30 degrees centigrade colder than it is.[9] With a continuing increase in greenhouse gases, there will be a continuing increase in average global temperature. The consequences of this include a general rise in sea level, bringing flooding to coastal areas, and changes in climate which will produce crop failures in some regions and add to the rate of species extinctions because some plants and animals will find it hard to adapt.

Indicators of the greenhouse effect can be found anywhere along the chain of cause-and-effect from emissions of green-house gases to their concentration in the atmosphere, to the resulting average temperature change, and then to measure-ments of the effect on sea level and other consequences. Since each step along the chain of cause-and-effect brings in additional influences and uncertainties, it is simplest to take measurements of the first stage as the main indicator, i.e. the rate of emissions.

Amongst the emission rates, the most important is the rate for the gas which makes the biggest contribution (roughly 50 per cent of the total) to the greenhouse effect: carbon dioxide. Carbon dioxide emissions can be measured in millions of metric tons per year.

Carbon dioxide in the atmosphere derives from two main sources. One is fossil fuel use, which in 1986 accounted for 97 per cent of emissions created by human activity (cement production accounted for most of the rest).[10] The other main source is described as 'changes in land use', which primarily means tropical deforestation, estimated to be 'contributing 30 per cent of the buildup of carbon dioxide in the global atmosphere'.[11] Since the rate of deforestation has already been proposed as an indicator, it is proposed now to add to this information a further indicator to cover emissions from fossil fuel use.

The proposed indicators of the greenhouse effect are therefore: net annual percentage rate of deforestation, and *carbon dioxide emissions from fossil fuel use, in millions of metric tons per year*.

DESERTIFICATION

In recent decades, growth in world food production has been faster than the growth in world population. This is an important success for agriculture. But in addition to the fact that many countries – mainly in Africa – have failed to achieve this, there is also a negative side for the successful countries. In many areas, food has been grown at enormous cost to the environment – principally, to the quality of the soil – and in the long term this may make it very difficult to sustain recent rates of growth in food output.

The benefits brought by world agriculture have already been referred to in the previous chapter, proposing as an indicator calorie supply as a percentage of minimum requirements – a figure which has shown a general increase over the past 20 years. The negative side is more difficult to measure, partly because a number of very different phenomena are involved. The Brundtland Report says: 'Short-sighted policies are leading to degradation of the agricultural resource base on almost every continent: soil erosion in North America, soil acidification in Europe; deforestation and desertification in Asia, Africa, and

Latin America; and waste and pollution of water almost everywhere. Within 40–70 years, global warming may cause the flooding of important coastal production areas.'[12]

This chapter has already referred to the problems of global warming and deforestation, and proposed relevant indicators. In addition, there is a need for indicators of soil erosion and/or desertification (perhaps annual rate of desertification, as a percentage of the area of a country), but here there is a problem of lack of reliable data. An article in *Scientific American* reported: 'in most of the world's regions, accurate estimates of degradative processes are not available. . . . The U.S. is the only country in the world that has reasonably accurate and comprehensive estimates of soil erosion and its effect on productivity'.[13] According to the Worldwatch Institute, 'only a few countries regularly monitor these losses [of topsoil]'.[14] In *The Threatening Desert*, Alan Grainger refers to 'a continuing lack of reliable data on the scale of desertification'.[15] 'According to one estimate, the area suffering from at least moderate desertification is at the most 20 million square kilometres (sq km); but another gives an area of 32 million sq km, almost a quarter of the earth's land surface. The only estimate we have of the rate of desertification is 202,460 sq km per annum. All of these estimates are known to be very inaccurate.'[16]

There seems to be no practical alternative to drawing the conclusion that no indicator can be proposed for the purposes of this book, because the data is not available. It is, however, desirable that the information be collected, because it is clear from famines, the movement of refugees, and estimates made in various local studies, that the situation is desperate in some parts of the world.

POPULATION

One major influence on the environment is the size of the human population. A number of different possible indicators can be used to measure what is happening to population, including total size of population, average annual increase in population, and average number of children per woman. The indicator I propose to highlight here, because it relates current increases in population to the total already in existence, is *average annual percentage rate of increase in population*.

Moving from the rate of increase in population to an assessment of the environmental impact of that increase is, however, a complex matter. On the one hand, population needs to be considered in relation to the levels of consumption and environmental impact per person in different countries. The impact on the world as a whole of an extra million Americans, for example, is far more than the impact of an extra million people in Bangladesh. On the other hand, the environmental impact needs to be considered in relation to the current state of the environment and resources for each country (including imports made available through trade). In this sense, it is easier for the USA to absorb a one million increase in its population than for Bangladesh to do so. At the current rate of increase, the world population grows by a million every four and a half days.

LONG-TERM RISK

The idea of 'sustainability' raises the question of whether economic benefits being derived from production now are at the expense of future generations. One way of living at the actual or potential expense of the future is to take major risks. The general build-up of toxic chemicals and radioactive materials in the biosphere is an important example of this, because in addition to their short-term effects on health, there is a long-term accumulation taking place which could have disastrous consequences far into the future.

Perhaps the most dangerous of materials currently accumulating is plutonium, a man-made substance which did not exist on Earth until 1940. It has a half-life of 24,400 years – which means that if the inventors of bows and arrows had created plutonium instead, that plutonium would still retain most of its radioactivity today.

The obvious type of indicator to choose here is one for quantity of plutonium in existence, but data is not available for all countries. Information is, however, available on *number of operable nuclear reactors*. Although different types of nuclear reactors vary in both the quantity of plutonium they produce, and in their design and safety records, this indicator has the advantage of simplicity. A nuclear reactor is much easier to visualize than are the units which would have to be used for more complex indicators, and the meaning of the numbers is therefore much easier to grasp.

The figures quoted in chapter 9 are for nuclear reactors able to produce electricity for the commercial electricity grid, on 31 December of the year indicated.

An indicator of pollution is another possibility, but it is difficult to find internationally comparable data because methods of measuring pollution vary; measurements of pollution differ enormously between different localities rather than providing meaningful overall national or regional averages; and there is often a lack of data for Third World countries.

ENERGY INTENSITY

Another important area to examine is the use of resources such as minerals and fossil fuels. Indicators might include measurements of: quantity of reserves and their rate of depletion; the proportion of resources used which derive from recycling; and the efficiency with which resources are used.

Energy plays a central role both in the economy itself and in its environmental impact, and by using units of energy (such as tons of coal equivalent) it is possible to combine in a single indicator data about a range of different resources.

An energy indicator which is already often quoted, especially in the USA, is the figure for 'energy intensity of GDP', defined as energy consumption per unit of GDP output, for example *energy consumption in metric tons of oil equivalent per million dollars of output*. If energy intensity falls, then economic growth can be compatible with a reduction in energy consumption.

Similar figures could be calculated for the relationship between GDP and the consumption of minerals and other resources, where again there is no inevitability about the connection between economic growth as measured by GDP or GNP, and growth in the consumption of resources.

CONCLUSIONS

This chapter has highlighted just five priority indicators. The view taken here of which are the most severe environmental problems the world faces could, of course, be challenged, and additional indicators could be added to give a fuller picture of the problems which have been discussed. Although the focus of this book is on finding the internationally most significant indicators, in most cases it would be appropriate for specific governments and communities to highlight additional indicators for the specific forms of resource depletion, pollution, and environmental degradation which particularly concern them.

The set of priority environmental indicators which has emerged from the 'seven criteria for a good indicator' set out in chapter 6, and from the discussion in this chapter, is as follows (the numbering is continued from the previous chapter):

12 Deforestation in square kilometres per year.
13 Carbon dioxide emissions from fossil fuel use, in millions of metric tons per year.
14 Average annual percentage rate of increase in population.
15 Number of operable nuclear reactors.
16 Energy consumption (in tons of oil equivalent) per million dollars of GDP.

In addition, there is an urgent need for more comprehensive data both on rates of species loss and rates of desertification.

9

DATA FOR FOURTEEN MAJOR COUNTRIES

This chapter uses the proposed priority indicators as a means of assessing the current state of fourteen major countries. As well as providing information about these countries, these statistics are the basis for the discussion in chapter 10 of the differences in practice between using economic indicators such as GNP and using the other indicators advocated in this book.

Of the fourteen countries selected for inclusion in this chapter, half are the members of the Group of Seven – the USA, Canada, Japan, France, West Germany, Italy, and the UK – which meet annually for economic summits, and together dominate international economic and financial organizations such as the International Monetary Fund and the World Bank. The other seven countries selected are those in the rest of the world estimated for the year 2000 to have the largest populations.[1] They are (in order of population): China, India, USSR, Indonesia, Brazil, Nigeria, and Bangladesh. These fourteen countries represent 66 per cent of the world's people, i.e. almost twice as many as all other countries put together. For more comprehensive sets of data, readers should refer to the sources quoted for this chapter at the end of the book.

The years for which information is quoted here are generally: 1970, 1980, and 1985; and where more recent information is available, the most recent available estimate has also been included. From the perspective of 1990 (when this book was completed), this represents the situation 20 years ago, 10 years ago, and 5 years ago, as well as the most up-to-date published information.

In attempting to compile this data, I have discovered that a great deal of it is not available, and so there are inevitably many gaps in the tables. Some of the reasons for these have already been referred to in chapters 7 and 8, in the course of discussing specific indicators.

DATA FOR FOURTEEN MAJOR COUNTRIES

Indicator 1: Net primary school enrolment ratio for girls

	1970	*1980*	*1985*	*Latest year*
USA		95	95	96 (1986)
Canada	93	96 (1981)		97 (1987)
Japan	99	100	100	100 (1986–8)
France	98	100	97	100 (1987)
West Germany	92	81	83	86 (1986)
Italy			96 (1984)	98 (1986–8)
UK	98	96	96	100 (1986)
Bangladesh	32	47	45	57 (1988)
China				91 (1986)
India	44			
Indonesia		83	96	96 (1986)
USSR				
Brazil				
Nigeria				85 (1986–8)

Main source: UNESCO Statistical Yearbooks.[2]

Indicator 2: Net primary school enrolment ratio for boys

	1970	*1980*	*1985*	*Latest year*
USA		94	94	95 (1986)
Canada	92	97 (1981)		97 (1987)
Japan	99	100	100	100 (1986–8)
France	98	100	97	100 (1987)
West Germany	88	79	81	84 (1986)
Italy			96 (1984)	97 (1986–8)
UK	98	95	95	100 (1986)
Bangladesh	62	76	63	67 (1988)
China				99 (1986)
India	69			
Indonesia		93	100	99 (1986)
USSR				
Brazil				
Nigeria				97 (1986–8)

Main source: UNESCO Statistical Yearbooks.[2]

ALTERNATIVE ECONOMIC INDICATORS

Indicator 3: Female illiteracy.
Female illiterate population as a percentage of total female
population, 15 years of age and over.

	1970	1980	1985
USA	1		
Canada			
Japan	1		
France	2		
West Germany			
Italy	7	5 (1981)	4
UK			
Bangladesh	88	80	78
China		49 (1982)	44
India	80	74 (1981)	71
Indonesia	58	42	35
USSR	3		
Brazil	37	27	23
Nigeria	86	77	69

Main source: UNESCO Statistical Yearbooks.[3]

Indicator 4: Male illiteracy.
Male illiterate population as a percentage of total male population, 15
years of age and over.

	1970	1980	1985
USA	1		
Canada			
Japan	1		
France	1		
West Germany			
Italy	5	3 (1981)	2
UK			
Bangladesh	64	57	57
China		21 (1982)	18
India	53		43
Indonesia	34	23	17
USSR	2		
Brazil	31	24	21
Nigeria	65	54	46

Main source: UNESCO Statistical Yearbooks.[3]

Indicator 5: Percentage rate of unemployment.
Using standard International Labour Organization definition.

	1970	1980	1985	1988
USA	5	7	7	5
Canada	6	8	11	8
Japan	1	2	3	3
France	3	6	10	10
West Germany	1	3	9	9
Italy	5	8	10	12
UK	3	7	12	8
Bangladesh				
China (urban areas only)		5	2	2 (1987)
India				
Indonesia				
USSR				
Brazil		4 (1981)	3	
Nigeria				

Main source: ILO *Year Books of Labour Statistics*.[4] Published data has been rounded up or down to the nearest whole number.

Indicator 6: Average daily calorie supply per person as a percentage of minimum requirement

	1970	1980	1985
USA	135 (1972)	139	140
Canada	128 (1972)	127	130
Japan	122	124	106
France	135 (1972)	134	142
West Germany	128 (1972)	133	133
Italy	126	150	143
UK	133 (1972)	132	129
Bangladesh	89	84	78
China	100	107	111
India	92	87	94
Indonesia	91	110	109
USSR	128	132	128
Brazil	104	109	107
Nigeria	89	91	92

Main source: *The State of the World's Children* (UNICEF).[5]

Indicator 7: Percentage of the population with access to
safe drinking water

	1970	1980	1985	1985–7
USA				
Canada				
Japan				
France			100	
West Germany				
Italy				
UK			100	
Bangladesh	45	39	46	46
China (urban areas only, tap water only)		81		85
India	17	42	56	57
Indonesia	3	23	38	38
USSR				
Brazil	55	72	77	78
Nigeria			38	46

Main source: United Nations Environment Programme *Environmental Data Report 1989/90.*[6]

Indicator 8: Telephones in use per thousand people

	1970	1980	1985
USA	583	788	
Canada	454	686	654 (1984)
Japan	193	460	555
France	172	459	608
West Germany	225	464	621
Italy	174	337	448
UK	251	477	524 (1984)
Bangladesh		1 (1979)	
China		4	6
India	2	4 (1979)	5
Indonesia	2	3	
USSR	45	89	110 (1986)
Brazil	21	62	84
Nigeria	1	2 (1977)	3

Source: United Nations *World Statistics in Brief.*[7]

Indicator 9: Income distribution.
Percentage share of household income received by the top 20 per cent
of households divided by percentage share received by the bottom 20
per cent.

	1970	1980	1985
USA	10 (1972)	8	10
Canada	8 (1969)	8 (1981)	
Japan	5 (1969)	4 (1979)	
France	11	8 (1975)	
West Germany	7 (1973)	5 (1978)	
Italy	9 (1969)	7 (1977)	
UK	6 (1973)	6 (1979)	7 (1982)
Bangladesh	7 (1973/4)	7 (1981/2)	
China (urban areas only)			3 (1984)
India	7 (1964/5)	7 (1975/6)	
Indonesia		7 (1976)	
USSR			
Brazil	33 (1972)	28 (1982)	
Nigeria			

Calculated from data in: *World Development Reports*.[8]

Indicator 10: Infant mortality rate.
Deaths of babies under 1 year of age per 1,000 live births.

	1970	1980	1985	1988
USA	20	13	11	10
Canada	19	11	8	7
Japan	13	7	6	5
France	18	10	8	8
West Germany	24	14	10	8
Italy	30	14	12	10
UK	18	12	9	9
Bangladesh	153	136	123	118
China		56	35	31
India	134	123	89	98
Indonesia	126	93	96	84
USSR	24	27	29	25
Brazil		77	67	62
Nigeria	154 (1965/6)	135	109	104

Main source: *World Development Reports*.[9]

Indicator 11: Under-5 mortality rate.
Deaths of babies and children under 5 years of age per 1,000 live births.

	1980	1985	1988
USA	16	13	13
Canada	13	10	8
Japan	12	9	8
France	13	11	10
West Germany	17	12	10
Italy	18	13	11
UK	16	12	11
Bangladesh	211	196	188
China	56	50	43
India	180	158	149
Indonesia	145	126	119
USSR	33	29	32
Brazil	103	91	85
Nigeria	198	182	174

Main source: *The State of the World's Children.*[10]

Indicator 12: Tropical deforestation rate.
Square kilometres per year.

	Late 1970s	1989	(1989 rate as % of existing area)
USA			
Canada			
Japan			
France			
West Germany			
Italy			
UK			
Bangladesh			
China			
India	2,600	4,000	(2.4%)
Indonesia	6,600	12,000	(1.4%)
USSR			
Brazil	14,500	50,000	(2.3%)
Nigeria	3,100	4,000	(14.3%)

Source: Report by Dr Norman Myers.[11]

DATA FOR FOURTEEN MAJOR COUNTRIES

Indicator 13: Carbon dioxide emissions from fossil fuel use in millions of metric tons per year.

	1965	1982	1985	1987
USA	935	1135	1186	
Canada	68	108	107	
Japan	101	226	244	
France	94	111	107	
West Germany	172	181	181	
Italy	49	88	101	
UK	169	141	148	
Bangladesh				
China	131	413	508	
India		105		
Indonesia				28
USSR	509	901	958	
Brazil		42		53
Nigeria				9

Various sources.[12]

Indicator 14: Population growth.
Average annual percentage rate of increase in population.

	1965–70	1975–80	1980–5	1986–2000 estimate
USA	1.1	1.1	1.0	0.6
Canada	1.7	1.2	1.1	0.7
Japan	1.1	0.9	0.7	0.5
France	0.8	0.4	0.6	0.4
West Germany	0.6	−0.1	−0.2	−0.3
Italy	0.6	0.4	0.3	0.1
UK	0.4	0.0	0.1	0.1
Bangladesh	2.7	2.8	2.6	2.5
China	2.6	1.4	1.2	1.4
India	2.3	2.1	2.2	1.8
Indonesia	2.3	2.1	2.1	1.8
USSR	0.9	0.9	0.9	0.7
Brazil	2.6	2.3	2.3	1.9
Nigeria	3.2	3.5	3.3	3.3

Main source: *World Population Prospects* (UN 1986).[13]

Indicator 15: Operable nuclear reactors

	1970	1980	1986
USA	13	68	100
Canada	1	9	18
Japan	4	23	34
France	3	17	49
West Germany	1	10	19
Italy	2	3	3
UK	25	32	38
Bangladesh	0	0	0
China	0	0	0
India	2	4	6
Indonesia	0	0	0
USSR	11	26	53
Brazil	0	1	1
Nigeria	0	0	0

Source: *World Resources 1988–89*.[14]

Indicator 16: Energy intensity.
Total primary energy requirement divided by GDP, in tonnes of oil equivalent per thousand dollars of GDP at constant 1980 prices and constant exchange rates.

	1973	1979	1985	1987
USA	0.76	0.71	0.58	0.56
Canada	0.89	0.85	0.77	0.74
Japan	0.41	0.36	0.29	0.28
France	0.32 (1970)	0.30 (1980)	0.28	0.28
West Germany	0.38	0.36	0.31	0.30
Italy	0.36	0.34	0.29	0.28
UK	0.44	0.40	0.35	0.33
Bangladesh				
China		1.89	1.25	
India		0.67	0.67 (1984)	
Indonesia				
USSR		1.04		1.04 (1986)
Brazil		0.54	0.58 (1984)	
Nigeria				

Main source: UNEP *Environmental Data Report 1989/90*.[15]

DATA FOR FOURTEEN MAJOR COUNTRIES

Additional indicators: Gross national product per capita in US dollars, and gross domestic product in billions of US dollars, for 1985.

	GNP per capita	GDP
USA	16,690	3,947
Canada	13,680	346
Japan	11,300	1,328
France	9,540	510
West Germany	10,940	625
Italy	6,520	359
UK	8,460	454
Bangladesh	150	16
China	310	266
India	270	176
Indonesia	530	86
USSR		
Brazil	1,640	188
Nigeria	800	75

Main source: World Development Report 1987.[16]

10

CONCLUSIONS

WHAT DOES THE DATA SHOW?

This book was being written when the Berlin Wall came down. Many people are proclaiming an end to the division of the world between 'East' and 'West'. But the North/South division of the planet remains. This division is the clearest feature of the data set out in chapter 9, and appears in the case of almost every indicator.

(1) and (2) Primary school enrolment There is a significant gap between the Group of Seven countries (USA, Canada, Japan, France, West Germany, Italy, and the UK) and the countries of the 'South' (Bangladesh, China, India, Indonesia, Brazil, Nigeria). In the southern countries, female enrolment ratios are lower than the corresponding figures for males.

(3) and (4) Illiteracy There is an enormous contrast between the countries of the 'North' (the Group of Seven countries plus the USSR) and those of the 'South'. Figures are generally not available for this indicator for the Northern countries, presumably because illiteracy is thought by most governments not to be a significant problem. Where they are available, the figures are far lower than corresponding figures for the South. Over time, the general trend is one of improvement. Male illiteracy rates are generally considerably lower than the corresponding figures for female illiteracy.

(5) Unemployment In this case, it is figures for the South which are difficult to get, generally because systems of employment are less formalized than in the North, with larger numbers of people involved in 'informal self-employment'. 1988 figures for Northern countries range from 12 per cent in Italy to 3 per cent in Japan. In most countries, unemployment reached a peak

in the mid 1980s and has fallen or stayed constant since then (only in Italy has it continued to rise).

(6) Calorie supply In the Southern countries, average calorie supply as a percentage of minimum requirements rose between 1970 and 1985 – with the exception of Bangladesh. In the Northern countries, there have recently been some falls, but in every case this has been from a 1980 position of at least 24 per cent above the minimum requirement, and so this probably also represents an improvement in nutrition. The gap between North and South is clear.

(7) Access to safe water Figures for the North are generally not available because this is not thought to be a significant problem (a view confirmed by the 100 per cent figures for France and the UK in 1985). There is a very marked contrast between North and South, and a general trend towards improvement in the South. Safety of water supplies is re-emerging as an issue in the North because of chemical pollutants.

(8) Telephones There has been a general rise in telephone use throughout the world, with a very striking contrast between North and South, the extremes being 788 telephones per thousand people in the USA in 1980 and 1 per thousand people for Bangladesh in 1979.

(9) Income distribution Here the contrast is between Brazil and everywhere else. There was a slight tendency towards reduced inequality during the 1970s, but in the two (Northern) countries where data is available, this has been reversed during the 1980s.

(10) Infant mortality rate The average 1988 figure for the Group of Seven countries is 8, whereas the average for the six Southern countries is 83. A general improvement has taken place in both North and South – except that the infant mortality rate has recently risen in India.

(11) Under-5 mortality rate Here there is a similar picture as for infant mortality (though U5MR in India has continued to fall).

(12) Tropical deforestation The rate of deforestation has increased greatly in recent years.

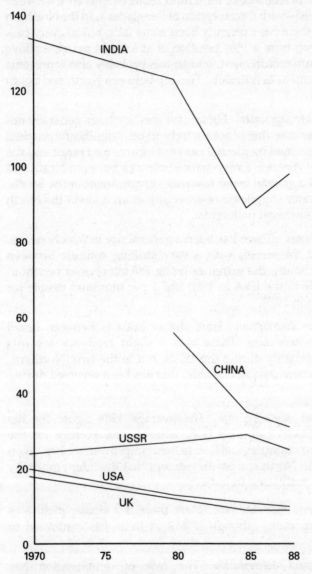

Figure 10.1 Infant mortality rate

(13) Carbon dioxide emissions from fossil fuels Here the figures for different countries are obviously related to their total fossil fuel use, giving the USA and USSR the highest rates of emissions. In general (despite the overall reduction in energy intensity shown by indicator 16) the pattern is one of an increase in carbon dioxide emissions. For the nine countries listed where data is available for both 1965 and 1985, total emissions from fossil fuel use have gone from 2.2 billion tons a year to 3.5 billion tons – an increase of 59 per cent in 20 years.

(14) Population growth The rate of growth in the six Southern countries in 1980–5 averaged 2.3 per cent, with the rate for the G7 averaging 0.5 per cent. Since 1965–70, there has been a general decline in the rate of increase in the population, with the fall being more marked in the North than in the South.

(15) Nuclear reactors The pattern is one of a general increase in the numbers of operable reactors. The six Southern countries listed had 7 nuclear reactors between them in 1986, compared to an average of 39 *each* for the eight Northern countries.

(16) Energy intensity The 1986/7 figures range from Japan, Italy, and France at 0.28 tons per thousand dollars of GDP to the USSR at 1.04. The general pattern is one of falling energy intensity.

THE GENERAL PICTURE

Who is right? Is the anti-growth view, that the state of the world is generally deteriorating, nearer to the truth than the pro-growth view which sees things are generally improving?

It depends, of course, on what indicators you use. With GNP and GNP per head as the key indicators, the pro-growthists appear to be proved correct. But with the wider range of priority indicators advocated in this book, a more complex picture emerges.

I've gone through the data in chapter 9, selecting the two latest readings (e.g. 1985 and 1988) for every country listed for each of the sixteen indicators, and counted where there have been

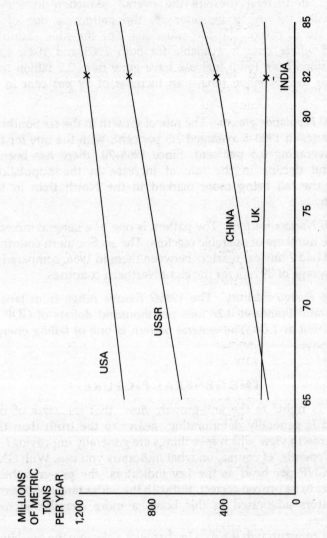

Figure 10.2 Carbon dioxide emissions from fossil fuel use

improvements and where things have got worse. I have counted figures going up as an improvement for indicators 1, 2, 6, 7, and 8, and down as an improvement for all the rest (calorie supply changes where they were already over 100 per cent have been counted as neither).

Out of 154 cases, there were 96 improvements, 29 worsenings, and 29 instances where things stayed the same. Dividing the indicators between social (1–11) and environmental (12–16) shows a marked difference between them. Amongst social indicators, 75 per cent of cases were improvements, only 8 per cent worsenings, and 17 per cent the same. *Every one of the eleven social indicators shows recent improvement overall* (i.e. more countries with improvements than with worsenings). Amongst environmental indicators, 38 per cent of cases were improvements, 39 per cent worsenings, and 23 per cent the same. *Three out of five environmental indicators show recent deterioration overall* (i.e. more countries with worsenings than with improvements).

Amongst the environmental indicators, a distinction can be made between 'causes' indicators and 'effects' indicators. The 'effects' indicators (tropical deforestation, carbon dioxide emissions, and nuclear reactors) all show a very clear deterioration in the situation (19 cases of things getting worse, 2 getting better). The 'causes' indicators (population growth and energy intensity) show a general improvement (2 worse, 18 better).

What are the implications of all this? There appear to be three main factors at work, each on a different timescale:

1 Social conditions are generally improving, and in the short term, this is likely to continue.
2 In the medium term, environmental deterioration threatens to put these social improvements into reverse. For example, growing desertification threatens current improvements in calorie supply; pollution will threaten current improvements in health.
3 In the long term, the outcome depends on whether the current improvements in environmental 'causes indicators' (such as energy intensity and rate of population growth) continue and are on a sufficiently big scale to put the environmental 'effects indicators' into reverse. This would allow the social indicators to resume their past trend of general improvement.

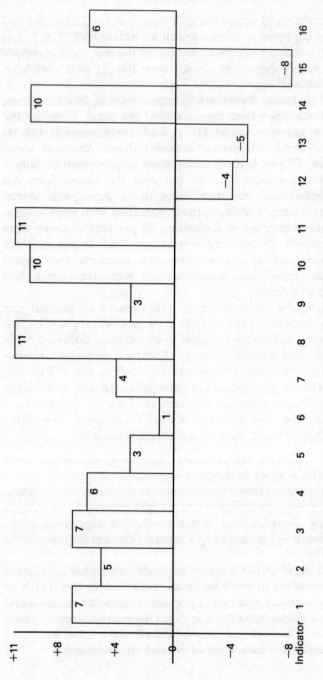

Figure 10.3 Number of countries with recent improvements minus number of countries with recent worsenings

The key difference between this conclusion and the views of the 'anti-growthists' and 'pro-growthists' introduced in the first chapter are as follows:

(1) The anti-growthists usually want to play down the significance of social improvements. The effect of this is to take away any sense that the world faces genuine dilemmas, and to make the issues appear much simpler than they really are. Just putting current economic and social development basically into reverse (assuming sufficient political support could be won for doing so) would have enormous costs. A more realistic project (not only in terms of political support, but also in terms of what the situation requires) is the attempt to combine as many of the human advantages of 'development' as possible with as few as possible of the environmental and human disadvantages. This will be a complex task, but hopefully not an impossible one.

(2) The pro-growthists' use of GNP and GNP growth rate gives a far too optimistic picture of the world. It plays down both distributional issues (about inequalities in health, wealth, and consumption) and environmental issues. Some indicators – such as illiteracy rates and access to safe drinking water – do show a close connection with GNP per head, but others do not, and some environmental indicators show a negative connection, i.e. prosperity bought at a high environmental cost. Though the pro-growthists rightly draw attention to benefits from increasing prosperity, such as falls in infant mortality rates, a continuation of economic growth in its present form into the future would be disastrous, because of the environmental costs involved. Statistics for the main indicators used by economists – GNP, balance of payments, inflation, etc. – do nothing to convey the nature and seriousness of the situation we face.

FUTURE DIRECTIONS

The most important need now is for policies and strategies to act on the causes of environmental impact – such as growth in population and inefficiency in energy use. Economics can play an important role in creating such policies and strategies *if* it is put back into its human and environmental context.

As part of the change that is required, there is a need for

change specifically in the field of indicators. I will finish by listing some possible ways of taking the argument for alternative economic indicators further. This could be achieved by the following:

(1) More accurate and *more comprehensive collection of data*, especially environmental data in countries particularly dependent on forest and other natural resources. There should be financial assistance to Third World countries, through the United Nations, for the development of more adequate systems for collecting and processing statistical information. The countries with the worst problems generally lack the resources necessary to monitor adequately the nature and location of those problems. Countries which are poor in most other ways tend also to be poor in data.

(2) *Publicity* for what the priority indicators show, particularly where currently only financial indicators are quoted and publicized. Fluctuations in infant mortality rates should be given more prominence than fluctuations in stock exchange prices. The aim should be to build up a public opinion and political system as sensitive to changes in social and environmental indicators as the financial markets now are to changes in financial indicators.

(3) The development of sets of indicators which reflect different *national, regional, and local priorities* (those in this book are intended to reflect global priorities).

(4) Organizations concerned with environment, development, and other issues, should make their own lists of priority indicators, which could then be compared and discussed, with the aim of developing consensus around a proposed set of alternative indicators, to be used as a basis for *political campaigning* for economies to be evaluated by a much wider range of indicators than at present.

(5) The development of *social and environmental auditing* and accounting for individual companies, local councils, and other organizations, in ways which connect up with the totals and averages presented by alternative economic indicators (in the same sort of way as firms' financial accounts link in with national income accounts at present).

(6) The further development of social *indicators to measure hard-to-define factors* such as democratic participation, the observance of human rights, the existence and strength of community life, and people's subjective feelings about their happiness and quality of life.

(7) Changes are necessary in the *machinery of government* of most countries in the world so that their economic policies can be shaped by indicators which reflect the social and environmental effects of the economy, and not just the economy itself seen in financial terms. This will involve restructuring Ministries of Finance, Economic Affairs, the Treasury, etc.

(8) The policies, activities, and statements of *international organizations* such as the International Monetary Fund, the World Bank, and the Group of Seven, should be monitored and criticized in the light of alternative economic indicators. Smug assessments of the world economic situation should be challenged with data about malnutrition, mass poverty, infant deaths, and desertification.

(9) In the short term, political support and pressure needs to be generated for *changes within the existing framework of national income accounting*, especially for the addition of figures for the value of unpaid work and the subtraction of figures for environmental depreciation. Although reforms within the existing framework are not the preferred strategy argued for in this book, they would nevertheless represent important improvements on the existing situation.

Narrowly financial criteria have ruled economic policy-making for too long. It is time to bring human and environmental realities back into economics.

NOTES AND REFERENCES

1 THE GROWTH DEBATE

1 E. Goldsmith, R. Allen, M. Allaby, J. Davoll, and S. Lawrence, *A Blueprint for Survival*, special issue of *The Ecologist*, January 1972, 2.
2 ibid., 3.
3 ibid., 38.
4 D. H. Meadows, D. L. Meadows, J. Randers, and W. Behrens III, *The Limits to Growth* (London: Pan, 1974), 23–4.
5 ibid., 124.
6 ibid., 126.
7 ibid., 127.
8 ibid., 136.
9 ibid., 183.
10 See, for example, ibid., 108. The implications of the distinction between industrial output growth and GNP growth are discussed in D. L. Meadows *et al.*, *Dynamics of Growth in a Finite World*, (Cambridge, Massachusetts: Wright – Allen Press, 1974), 204–8.
11 Meadows, Meadows, Randers, and Behrens, op. cit., 171.
12 ibid., 183.
13 E. F. Schumacher, *Small is Beautiful* (London: Sphere, 1974), 122–3.
14 ibid., 246.
15 ibid., 23.
16 ibid., 35–6.
17 A. Crosland, *A Social Democratic Britain* (London: Fabian Society, 1971), 5.
18 ibid., 6.
19 W. Beckerman, *In Defence of Economic Growth* (London: Cape, 1974), inside front cover.
20 ibid., 242.
21 ibid., 247.
22 ibid., 100.
23 R. Whelan, *Mounting Greenery* (Warlingham: Institute of Economic Affairs Education Unit, 1989), 31.
24 ibid., 29.
25 ibid., 15.
26 ibid., 19.
27 ibid., 17.

28 ibid., 46.
29 ibid., 57–8.
30 World Commission on Environment and Development, *Our Common Future* (Oxford: Oxford University Press, 1987), 30.
31 ibid., 343.
32 ibid., xii.
33 ibid., 43.
34 D. Pearce, A. Markandya, and E. B. Barbier, *Blueprint for a Green Economy* (London: Earthscan, 1989).
35 The Green Party, *Manifesto for a Sustainable Society* (London, 1988), 1.
36 H. S. D. Cole, C. Freeman, M. Jahoda, and K. Pavitt (eds), *Thinking About The Future* (London: Chatto & Windus, 1973). See also S. Cole, 'Global Models', in *Futures*, August 1987, 403–30.
37 See P. Ekins (ed.), *The Living Economy* (London: Routledge & Kegan Paul, 1986); J. Robertson, *Future Wealth* (London: Cassell, 1989); M. Jacobs, *The Green Economy* (London: Pluto, forthcoming).
38 Goldsmith *et al.*, op. cit., 2.
39 Schumacher, op. cit., 40.

2 THE ORIGINS OF NATIONAL INCOME ACCOUNTING

1 Quoted in E. Roll, *A History of Economic Thought* (London: Faber & Faber, 4th edition, 1973), 100.
2 D. Patinkin, *Anticipations of the General Theory?* (Oxford: Basil Blackwell, 1982), 246.
3 ibid., 240.
4 J. M. Keynes, *The General Theory of Employment Interest and Money* (London: Macmillan, 1939), 245.
5 ibid., 127.
6 J. M. Keynes, 'The Income and Fiscal Potential of Great Britain', in *The Economic Journal*, December 1939, reprinted in D. Moggridge (ed.) *The Collected Writings of John Maynard Keynes* (Cambridge: Cambridge University Press, 1978), vol. XXII, 52.
7 J. M. Keynes, Letter to F. A. Keynes, 14.4.41, ibid., 354.

3 PROBLEMS OF NATIONAL INCOME ACCOUNTING

1 See S. Lewenhak, *The Revaluation of Women's Work* (London: Croom Helm, 1988); M. Waring, *If Women Counted* (London: Macmillan, 1989).
2 A. J. Taylor, *The Standard of Living in Britain in the Industrial Revolution* (London: Methuen, 1975), xxxix.
3 See F. Hirsch, *Social Limits to Growth* (London: Routledge & Kegan Paul, 1977).

4 POSSIBLE REFORMS IN NATIONAL INCOME ACCOUNTING

1 *Hansard* 11.4.89.
2 See W. D. Nordhaus and J. Tobin, 'Is Growth Obsolete?', *Economic Growth, Fiftieth Anniversary Colloquium*, New York, National Bureau of Economic Research, 1972, vol. 5. Reprinted in R. Dorfman and N. S. Dorfman (eds), *Economics of the Environment* (New York: Norton, 1977), 485.
3 See C. Leipert, 'Social Costs of Economic Growth', *Journal of Economic Issues*, March 1986; R. Hueting and C. Leipert, *Economic Growth, National Income and the Blocked Choices for the Environment* (West Berlin, International Institute for Environment and Society, 1987); R. Repetto, 'Resources and Economic Accounts', paper for Organisation for Economic Co-operation and Development (Paris, 1988); Y. J. Ahmad, S. El Serafy, and E. Lutz (eds), *Environmental Accounting for Sustainable Development* (Washington DC: World Bank, 1989).
4 Nordhaus and Tobin, op. cit., 482.
5 ibid., 483.
6 See Ahmad, El Serafy, and Lutz, op. cit.; D. Pearce, A. Markandya, and E. B. Barbier, *Blueprint for a Green Economy* (London: Earthscan Publications, 1989), chapter 4.
7 T. S. Kuhn, *The Structure of Scientific Revolutions* (Chicago: The University of Chicago Press, 1962).

5 GROWTH AND PROGRESS

1 K. Kumar, *Prophecy and Progress* (Harmondsworth: Penguin, 1978), 31.
2 A. Smith, *The Wealth of Nations* (Harmondsworth: Penguin, 1974), 480.

6 THE GOOD INDICATOR

1 M. Abrams, 'Subjective Social Indicators', in M. Nissell (ed.), *Social Trends* No. 4, (London: Central Statistical Office, 1973), 35.
2 J. Hall, 'Subjective Measures of Quality of Life in Britain: 1971 to 1975', in E. J. Thompson (ed.), *Social Trends* No. 7 (London: Central Statistical Office, 1976), 47–60.
3 Abrams, op. cit., 41.
4 Hall, op. cit., 51.
5 A. Findlay, A. Morris, and R. Rogerson, *Quality of Life in British Cities* (Glasgow: University of Glasgow Department of Geography, 1988), 2, 4.
6 *Guardian*, 20 May 1987.

7 SOCIAL INDICATORS

1 J. A. Brewster, M. Paden, R. Kwartin, L. Wenzel, J. Adcock, J. Wayem, N. Burns, and E. Davey, *World Resources 1988–89* (New York: Basic Books, 1988), 262.

2 J. P. Grant, *The State of the World's Children* (Oxford: Oxford University Press, 1988), 84.

3 R. Dixon-Mueller and R. Anker, *Assessing Women's Economic Contributions to Development* (Geneva: International Labour Office, 1988), 65.

4 R. Carr-Hill and J. Lintott, 'Social Indicators for Popular Planning', in P. Ekins (ed.), *The Living Economy* (London: Routledge & Kegan Paul, 1986), 152.

5 Dixon-Mueller and Anker, op. cit., 47.

6 L. Goldschmidt-Clermont, *Unpaid Work in the Household* (Geneva: International Labour Office, 1982); L. Goldschmidt-Clermont, *Economic Evaluations of Unpaid Household Work: Africa, Asia, Latin America, and Oceania* (Geneva: International Labour Office, 1987). See also S. Lewenhak, *The Revaluation of Women's Work* (London: Croom Helm), 1988.

7 Brewster, op. cit., 262.

8 ibid., 251.

9 Socio-Economic Data Division, International Economics Department, The World Bank, *Social Indicators of Development 1988* (Baltimore: Johns Hopkins University Press, 1988), 7.

10 ibid.

11 *Development of Indicators for Monitoring Progress Towards Health for All by the Year 2000* (Geneva: World Health Organization, 1981), 68.

12 T. Hancock, 'Towards a Healthier Economy: health-based indicators of economic progress', paper for The Other Economic Summit conference, London, 1985, 11–12.

13 K. Newland, *Infant Mortality & the Health of Societies* (Washington DC: Worldwatch Institute, 1981), quoted by Hancock, op. cit., 10.

14 J. P. Grant, *The State of the World's Children 1990* (Oxford: Oxford University Press, 1990), 91.

8 ENVIRONMENTAL INDICATORS

1 See J. Maini, P. Garvåsjordet, H. Viggo Saebø, P. Cornière, M. Lenco, *Information and Natural Resources* (Paris: Organization for Economic Co-operation and Development, 1986); and K. H. Alfsen, T. Bye, and L. Lorentsen, *Natural Resource Accounting and Analysis: The Norwegian Experience 1978–1986* (Oslo: Central Bureau of Statistics of Norway, 1987).

2 L. R. Brown, W. Chandler, A. Durning, C. Flavin, L. Heise, J. Jacobson, S. Postel, C. Shen, L. Starke, and E. Wolf, *State of the World 1988* (New York: Norton 1988), 84.

3 N. Myers, *Deforestation Rates in Tropical Forests and Their Climatic Implications* (London: Friends of the Earth, 1989), 8.
4 E. O. Wilson, 'Threats to Biodiversity', in *Scientific American*, September 1989, 60.
5 Brown, op. cit., 105.
6 Wilson, op. cit., 64.
7 World Commission on Environment and Development, *Our Common Future* (Oxford: Oxford University Press, 1987), 151.
8 G. O. Barney (ed.) *The Global 2000 Report to the President* (Harmondsworth: Penguin 1982), 331.
9 S. Boyle, L. Taylor, and I. Brown, *Solving the Greenhouse Dilemma* (London: Association for the Conservation of Energy 1989), 4.
10 Calculated from United Nations Environment Programme, *Environmental Data Report* (Oxford: Basil Blackwell, 1989), 17.
11 Myers, op. cit., 1.
12 World Commission on Environment and Development, op. cit., 125.
13 P. R. Crosson and N. J. Rosenberg, 'Strategies for Agriculture', in *Scientific American*, September 1989, 78.
14 Brown, op. cit., 5.
15 A. Grainger, *The Threatening Desert* (London: Earthscan, 1990), xii.
16 ibid., 3.

9 DATA FOR FOURTEEN MAJOR COUNTRIES

1 *World Population Prospects* (New York: United Nations, 1986). 'Medium variant estimate' for 2000.
2 *Statistical Yearbooks* (Paris: UNESCO, 1984 and 1989). J. P. Grant, *The State of the World's Children* (Oxford: Oxford University Press, 1990).
3 *Statistical Yearbooks* (Paris: UNESCO, 1982 and 1989). *World Statistics in Brief* (New York: United Nations, 1987). J. P. Grant, *The State of the World's Children* (Oxford: Oxford University Press, 1988).
4 *Year Book of Statistics 1988* (Geneva: International Labour Organization). *Bulletin of Labour Statistics 1989 (4)* (Geneva: International Labour Organization). *OECD Economic Outlook* December 1989, Paris, OECD.
5 *The State of the World's Children 1984. The State of the World's Children 1988.* World Bank, *World Tables* (Baltimore: Johns Hopkins University Press, 1980).
6 United Nations Environment Programme, *Environmental Data Report 1989/90* (Oxford: Basil Blackwell, 1989). J. A. Brewster, *World Resources 1988–89* (New York: Basic Books, 1988). *The State of the World's Children 1990.*
7 *World Statistics in Brief* (New York: United Nations, 1981, 1986, and 1988).
8 World Bank, *World Development Report 1980* (New York: Oxford University Press). *World Development Report 1987. World Development Report 1988. World Resources 1988–89.* World Bank, *Social*

Indicators of Development 1988 (Baltimore: Johns Hopkins University Press).

9 *World Development Report 1982. World Development Report 1987. World Health Statistics Annual 1970* (Geneva: World Health Organization, 1973). *Demographic Yearbook 1974* (New York: United Nations, 1975). *Social Indicators of Development 1989. World Tables, 1980. The State of the World's Children 1990.*

10 *The State of the World's Children 1987. The State of the World's Children 1990.*

11 N. Myers, *Deforestation Rates in Tropical Forests and Their Climatic Implications* (London: Friends of the Earth, 1989).

12 *World Resources 1988–89. Environmental Data Report 1989/90.* L. R. Brown *State of The World 1988* (New York: Norton). *Financial Times*, 16.3.90.

13 *World Population Prospects, 1986. World Development Report 1987. World Development Report 1988.*

14 *World Resources 1988–89.*

15 *Environmental Data Report 1989/90.* Calculated from *OECD Environmental Data Compendium 1989,* Paris.

16 *World Development Report 1987. The State of the World's Children 1988.*

INDEX

Abrams, Mark 52
adjusted national product 34–5, 39–41, 50, 65
Assessing Women's Economic Contributions to Development (ILO) 57–8

Bangladesh 75–89 *passim*
barter 23
Beckerman, Wilfred 7–9
Blueprint for a Green Economy (Pearce Report) 13
Blueprint for Survival (*The Ecologist*) 1–2; indicators used in 5, 14, 21
Brandt Report 11
Brazil 75–89 *passim*
Brundtland, Gro Harlem 11–12
Brundtland Report (1987) 11–13, 69, 70–1

calorie supply 59–60, 64, 70, 79, 87, 91
Canada 75–89 *passim*; environmental accounting in 66
carbon dioxide emissions 69–70, 83, 89, 90, 91
China 75–89 *passim*
circumstances: and needs 24–5
class, social: and growth debate 6–7, 8; and income distribution 43
Condorcet, Marquis de 42–3

consumer choice: and national income accounting 30, 39
consumption 59–60, 64, 79–80, 87
coral reefs 69
Costs of Economic Growth (Mishan) 5
Counting Women's Unremunerated Work Bill (1989; UK) 34
Crosland, Anthony 6–7

data collection 49, 94
death rate: crude 61–2; infant 62–3, 64, 81, 87, 88, 93, 94, 95; under-five 63–4, 82, 87
defense expenditure 37–8
deforestation, tropical 66–7, 82, 89, 91; and greenhouse effect 70; and species extinction 68–9
Deforestation Rates in Tropical Forests and Their Climatic Implications (Myers) 67
depreciation: of capital goods 20, 36, 39; environmental 26–7, 35–7, 39, 40, 41, 95; of human capital 27–8, 29, 37; and positional goods 28; of possessions 26, 40
desertification 70–1, 91, 95
development theories 49
domestic labour, unpaid 19, 22–3, 33–4, 39, 57–8

'ecological demand' 1

Ecologist, The: A Blueprint for Survival 1–2, 5, 14, 21
Ecology Party (UK) 2
economics, history of 42–6
education 55–7, 64, 77, 86
electricity generation 73
energy: consumption 60; intensity 73, 84, 89, 91
environmental accounting 65–6, 94
environmental depreciation 26–7, 35–7, 39, 40, 41, 95
environmental indicators 48, 66–74, 91–3; international comparison of 82–4, 89; novelty of 49
environmental wealth 26–7
ethics: and economics 43–4, 46
evaluation of indicators 21, 48
exchange rates 25

Fabian Society 6–7
food consumption 59–60, 64, 70, 91, 95; international comparison of 79, 87
forests *see* deforestation
fossil fuels: carbon dioxide emissions from 70, 83, 89, 90, 91; and energy intensity 73
France 75–89 *passim*; environmental accounting in 66

GDP (gross domestic product): definition of 19–20; energy intensity of 73, 84, 89, 91; international comparison of 85; as valid indicator 1, 14–15, 18–19
General Theory of Employment Interest and Money (Keynes) 17
Germany, West 75–89 *passim*
Glasgow University 53
Global 2000 Report to the President 69
global warming 69
GNP (gross national product): additions to 33–5; and adjusted national product 39; and consumption 59; definition of 19–20; international comparison of 85; and progress 45; reforms of 33–41; subtractions from 35–7; and success 21; as valid indicator 5–6, 14, 15, 18–19, 21–32, 89, 93
Goldsmith, Edward 1
Gordon, Mildred 34
Grainger, Alan 71
Green Party (UK) 2, 13
greenhouse effect 69–70
Group of Seven 75–89 *passim*, 95
growth, economic: case against 1–6, 89, 93; case for 6–11, 89, 93; and energy resources 73 and progress 42, 45–6; *see also* national income accounting

Hall, John 52, 53
health: dangers 35; indicators 61–4, 81–2, 87, 88; services 38
Hirsch, Fred 5
housework, unpaid 19, 22–3, 33–4, 39, 57–8
human capital 27–8, 29, 37
'human economics' 44, 45, 46–7; *see also* social indicators

illiteracy 56–7, 64, 78, 86, 93
imputed value 26, 40
In Defence of Economic Growth (Beckerman) 7–9
income: distribution 24, 31, 39, 40, 43, 60–1, 64; (international comparison of 81, 87); and housework 19, 22–3, 33–4; and output 22–3
India 75–89 *passim*
Indonesia 75–89 *passim*
industrialization: and economic growth 22–3
infant mortality rate 62–3, 64, 93; international comparison of 81, 87, 88; publicity for 94, 95
Institute of Economic Affairs 9–11
intermediate output 37–8
Intermediate Technology Development Group 5
international comparability 51, 53

International Labour Organization 57–8, 59
International Monetary Fund 75, 95
'Is Growth Obsolete?' (Nordhaus and Tobin) 37
Italy 75–89 *passim*

Japan 75–89 *passim*
Jevons, William 44

Keynes, John Maynard 17–18
Kuhn, Thomas 41

leisure time: and household activity 34; and national income accounting 29, 34–5
life expectancy at birth 62
Limits to Growth (Meadows *et al.*) 2–4, 5, 14–15; criticism of 8, 13
literacy 55–7, 64, 78, 86, 93
luxury goods 31

Malthus, Thomas Robert 43
marginal utility of money, diminishing 31
market forces 8, 9
Marshall, Alfred 44
Marx, Karl 43
Massachusetts Institute of Technology 1, 2
mathematics: and economics 44
Meadows, Dennis 2
Mill, John Stuart 43
mineral reserves: depletion of 2, 73; and energy intensity 73; as environmental wealth 27, 36
Mishan, E.J. 5
morality: and economics 43–4, 46
Mounting Greenery (Whelan) 9–11
Movement for Survival 2
Myers, Norman 67

national income accounting and environmental accounting 65; origins of 16–18; possible reforms of 33–41, 95; problems of 21–32, 47, 57–8; and progress 45
'natural economics' 45, 46–7; *see also* environmental indicators
needs: and circumstances 24–5
New Economics 13
Nigeria 75–89 *passim*
NNP (net national product) 20, 36, 39
non-money transactions: inside the household 19, 22–3, 33–4, 39, 57–8; outside the household 23, 34, 39
Nordhaus, W.D. 37
North/South division 86–9
Norway, environmental accounting in 65–6
novelty of indicators 49
nuclear reactors 72–3, 84, 89, 91

Organization for Economic Co-operation and Development 59
Our Common Future (Brundtland Report) 11–13, 69, 70–1
output: and income 22–3; and welfare 23–31
ozone layer, public concern about 54

Patinkin, Don 16–17
'Paying for the War' (Keynes) 17
Pearce Report (1989) 13
Petty, Sir William 16
plutonium 72–3
policies corresponding to indicators 48–9
political economy 43–4; renewal of 46
politics, green 9–10, 13, 93, 94, 95
pollution 8, 91; indicator of 73
population growth 14, 43, 71–2, 83, 89, 91; differing reasons for 24–5; environmental impact of 72
positional goods 28, 35
possessions 26, 40; *see also* wealth
primary school enrolment 56, 64, 77, 86

production, 'inefficiency' in 30–1
progress: and economic growth 42–6
public opinion 52–4, 94
publicity 94

Quality of Life in British Cities 53
quality of life at work 28, 29, 35

raw materials 37, 44–5
religion: and growth debate 4–5, 10–11
rent, imputed 26
Ricardo, David 43
risks, long-term 72–3

Saint-Simon, Henri 43
satisfaction, personal 52–4
school enrolment ratios 56, 64, 77, 86
Schumacher, E.F. 4–5, 15
science: and economics 42–3, 44
Scientific American 71
Sketch for an Historical Picture of the Progress of the Human Mind (Condorcet) 42–3
Small is Beautiful (Schumacher) 4–5, 15
Smith, Adam 43
social accounting 94
Social Democratic Britain (Fabian Society) 6–7
social indicators 48, 55–64, 91–3; further development of 94–5; international comparison of 77–82, 86–7; novelty of 49
social issues: and growth debate 2, 4–5, 6–7
Social Limits to Growth (Hirsch) 5
Social Trends 52–3
Soil Association 5
soil erosion 70–1
species extinction 67–9; and greenhouse effect 69
State of the World 1988 66–7
stocks: and GNP 25–8
subjective indicators 52–4
'success', indicators of 21, 48
sustainable development 12–13

sustainable national income 40–1

taxation: evasion of 23; and pollution 8
Taylor, A.J. 22–3
technology: and economics 42–3
telephone use 60, 64, 80, 87
Thinking About The Future (Cole et al.) 13
Threatening Desert (Grainger) 71
Tobin, J. 37
tropical rainforests, depletion of 66–7, 82, 89, 91; and greenhouse effect 70; and species extinction 68–9

under-five mortality rate 63–4, 82, 87
unemployment 58–9, 64, 79, 86–7
United Kingdom 75–89 *passim*; national income accounting in 16, 17–18
United Nations: Children's Fund (UNICEF) 63–4; Conference on the Environment (1972) 2; and data collection 94; Decade for Women (1975–85) 34; Educational Scientific and Cultural Organization (UNESCO) 56; Food and Agriculture Organization 59, 67; Population Division and Statistical Office 62, 63; World Commission on Environment and Development 11
United States 75–89 *passim*; national income accounting in 16
unpaid labour 19, 22–3, 33–4, 39, 57–8, 64, 95
USSR 75–89 *passim*

value 18–19; imputed 26, 40

water, safe drinking 60, 64, 80, 87, 93
wealth 26, 40; distribution of 61, 64; environmental 26–7
Wealth of Nations (Smith) 43

welfare: GNP as indicator of 21–2;
  inefficient provision of 29–31,
  39–40; and output 23–31
Whelan, Robert 9–11
Wilson, E.O. 68–9
women: education and literacy of
  56, 57, 64, 77, 78, 86; work done
  by 22, 33–4, 39, 57–8

work 57–8, 64; unpaid 19, 22–3,
  33–4, 39, 57–8, 64, 95; see also
  unemployment
World Bank 60–1, 75, 95
World Health Organization 59,
  60, 63
Worldwatch Institute 63, 66–7, 71